Personalizing Learning Through Voice and Choice

Adam Garry
Amos Fodchuk
Lauren Hobbs

Solution Tree | Press

a division of
Solution Tree

555 North Morton Street
Bloomington, IN 47404
800.733.6786 (toll free) / 812.336.7700
FAX: 812.336.7790

Email: info@SolutionTree.com
SolutionTree.com

Visit **go.SolutionTree.com/instruction** to download the free reproducibles in this book.

Printed in the United States of America

21   20   19   18   17   1   2   3   4   5

Library of Congress Cataloging-in-Publication Data

Names: Garry, Adam, author. | Fodchuk, Amos, author. | Hobbs, Lauren, author.
Title: Personalizing learning through voice and choice / Adam Garry, Amos
    Fodchuk, and Lauren Hobbs.
Description: Bloomington, IN : Solution Tree Press, [2018] | Series:
    Solutions | Includes bibliographical references.
Identifiers: LCCN 2017023978 | ISBN 9781935542179 (perfect bound)
Subjects: LCSH: Individualized instruction. | Student participation in
    curriculum planning.
Classification: LCC LB1031 .G378 2018 | DDC 371.39/4--dc23 LC record available at https://lccn.loc
    .gov/2017023978

Solution Tree
Jeffrey C. Jones, CEO
Edmund M. Ackerman, President

Solution Tree Press
President and Publisher: Douglas M. Rife
Editorial Director: Sarah Payne-Mills
Art Director: Rian Anderson
Managing Production Editor: Caroline Cascio
Senior Production Editor: Tonya Maddox Cupp
Senior Editor: Amy Rubenstein
Copy Editor: Ashante K. Thomas
Proofreader: Miranda Addonizio
Text and Cover Designer: Laura Cox
Editorial Assistants: Jessi Finn and Kendra Slayton

Acknowledgments

To my amazing family and loving wife, who supported me along this journey. In continued memory of my son Max.

—Adam

To my loving family, friends, and colleagues who love and support without condition. Katy, you are my partner and best friend.

—Amos

To my better half and my boys, who continue to make Taco Tuesday the best day of the week.

—Lauren

Solution Tree Press would like to thank the following reviewers:

James Cantonwine
Science, Physical Education, and Health Specialist
Evergreen Public Schools
Vancouver, Washington

Nicholas Ganster
Principal
Marion Junior-Senior High School
Marion, New York

Kirstin Girard
Principal
Dakota Prairie Elementary School
Brookings, South Dakota

Clint Heitz
Instructional Coach
Bettendorf Community Schools
Bettendorf, Iowa

Lori Hower
Technology Integration Coach
Ottawa High School
Ottawa, Kansas

Rachel Pierson
STEM Teacher
Janesville-Waldorf-Pemberton
  Elementary School
Janesville, Minnesota

Bruce Preston
Assistant Superintendent of
  Curriculum and Personnel
Howell Township
  Public Schools
Howell, New Jersey

Visit **go.SolutionTree.com/instruction** to download the free reproducibles in this book.

Table of Contents

Chapter 3: Empowering Learner Voice and Choice at Scale

Epilogue: The Personalized Approach

References and Resources

About the Authors

 **Adam Garry** is a former elementary school teacher and is Dell's director of global education strategy. He has presented at conferences around the world, including for the International Society for Technology in Education (ISTE), and has delivered keynotes across the United States and the Caribbean. He has a strong following on Twitter.

Over the years he has consulted in school districts across the United States on personalized learning, school transformation, professional development, 21st century skills, technology integration, curriculum and instruction, and leadership. He was also one of the facilitators for the Partnership for 21st Century Learning professional development affiliates program and ISTE's School 2.0 workshops.

Adam received a bachelor's degree in elementary education from the University of South Florida, a master's degree in teaching and learning with a technology emphasis from Framingham State College, and a certificate in administration and supervision from Johns Hopkins University.

To learn more about Adam's work, follow @agarry22 on Twitter.

Amos Fodchuk is president of Advanced Learning Partnerships (ALP), an educational consulting firm with active partnerships across the United States and in Canada. With his team, Amos has earned a rich record of success in the co-development and scale-up of innovative learning models with school districts, universities, corporations, and foundations, as well as state and federal government agencies.

A teaching veteran, Amos has earned over twenty local, state, and national awards for excellence and innovation in U.S. public education. Among his many distinctions, he is a National Board–certified teacher, Fulbright Scholar to the People's Republic of China, and two-time teacher of the year within Virginia Beach City Public Schools. Amos has led ALP since 2009 and actively supports executive teams through multiyear strategic consulting engagements. He remains active in the classroom, collaboratively planning, co-teaching, and innovating alongside educators and his team members.

Amos lives in Chapel Hill, North Carolina, with his wife, Katy, and their two children, Ansel and Evelyn. An avid cook and musician, he loves to explore United States and other cultures through these media with friends, family, and anyone else with whom his path may cross.

He earned his bachelor's degree in education at the University of Alberta, Canada, and his master's degree in literacy at California State University, Sacramento.

To learn more about Amos's work, follow @Amos_ALP on Twitter.

Lauren Hobbs is a former teacher and an experienced educator who has led, designed, and monitored teaching and learning initiatives throughout the educational landscape. She has experience developing curriculum, assessment, and instructional assets within large districts to support problem-based, student-centered learning initiatives and her passion for creativity led to designing and implementing programs to build executive function and 21st century skills using innovative assets for students of poverty.

As an education strategist for Dell, Lauren continues to support districts and institutions throughout the United States, consulting in designing transformational learning models that empower leaders, teachers, and learners throughout the process. She has presented at national and statewide conferences and authored articles on topics such as personalized learning, developing failing forward mindsets, innovation, and professional learning.

Living in Tampa, Florida, with her husband Cole and their two boys, Jackson and Parker, Lauren loves exploring the outdoors and traveling with her family.

Lauren earned her bachelor's degree in elementary education and her master's degree in curriculum and instruction from Florida State University.

To learn about Lauren's work, follow @laurhobbs on Twitter.

To book Adam Garry, Amos Fodchuk, or Lauren Hobbs for professional development, contact pd@SolutionTree.com.

Foreword

By William M. Ferriter

Can I ask you a tough question? How many students in your classrooms are truly satisfied with the learning spaces you have created for them? If your students reflect the national average, the answer is bound to be discouraging. Fewer than four in ten high schoolers report being engaged in their classes, and students often list boredom as the primary reason for dropping out of school (Busteed, 2013). Over 70 percent of students who don't graduate report having lost interest by ninth grade and, worse yet, the majority of dropouts are convinced that motivation is all that prevented them from earning a diploma (Azzam, 2007).

These numbers are troubling for anyone passionate about schools. They indicate systemic failure on the part of practitioners to inspire learners and warn us of the immediate need to transform education—a warning that school leadership expert and series contributor Scott McLeod (2014) issues:

> If we truly care about preparing kids for life and work success—*we need schools to be different.* If economic success increasingly means moving away from routine cognitive work, schools need to also move in that direction. If our analog, ink-on-paper information landscapes outside of school have been superseded by environments that are digital and online and hyperconnected and mobile, our information landscapes inside of school also should reflect those shifts. If our students' extracurricular learning opportunities often are richer and deeper than what they experience in their formal educational settings, it is time for us to catch up.

Scott is right, isn't he? Our schools really do need to catch up if they are going to remain relevant in a world where learning is more important than schooling—and catching up can only start when we are willing to rethink everything. We need to push aside the current norms defining education—that teachers are to govern, direct, and evaluate student work; that mastering content detailed in predetermined curricula is the best indicator of student success; that assessment and remediation are more important than feedback and reflection; that the primary reason for investing in tools and technologies is to improve on existing practices. It's time to implement notions that better reflect the complexity of the world in which we live.

That is the origin of this series. It is my attempt to give a handful of the most progressive educators that I know a forum for detailing what they believe it will take to *make schools different*. Each book encourages readers to question their core beliefs about what teaching and learning look like in action. More important, each title provides readers with practical steps and strategies for reimagining their day-to-day practices. Here's your challenge: no matter how unconventional these ideas, steps, and strategies may seem at first, and no matter how uncomfortable they make you feel, find a way to take action. There is no other way to create the learning spaces that your students deserve.

Introduction

Defining Moments and Defining Terms

We all experience defining moments that fill us with wonder, excitement, joy, or sadness. Those defining moments drive our thinking and form who we are as people, as parents, and as professionals. Adam can pinpoint one of his defining moments. It happened when his son, Michael, started high school. After Michael explained an assignment he was working on, Adam asked *why* he had to do the work. Michael responded with, "I don't know, Dad. I just go to school, do what they tell me, and come home."

Stories like these reinforce schools' need to transform to truly engage students in learning. As muddled as change can feel to educators, one thing remains clear: students will be invested in their learning if we empower them to help design their learning. What is the challenge in this for us educators? Figuring out what happens to systems when students and parents know that there's more than one path to learning. Before addressing systems, educators must agree on a common language. In this book, that means defining personalized learning. Beyond that, we help you decide how you might best use this book.

Consuming Personalized Content

In 2004, Blockbuster Video was a hub of in-home movie nights (Harress, 2013). Did you load up the car, drive miles to the store, peruse the aisles to select a video, and bring back the movie you chose? Did you frantically search the return bins looking for a favorite film that wasn't on the shelf? Blockbuster Video was so dominant in the video-renting business it didn't appear that anyone could steal its market share (Harress, 2013). National chains like Hollywood Video and Movie Gallery, and a bevy of local mom-and-pop video shops, tried. They were emulating the same business model Blockbuster had capitalized on.

What toppled the movie-rental monster? DVDs, high-speed internet connections, and the determination of streaming video companies like Netflix (Satell, 2014). Allowing customers to create a queue and receive movies via mail removed the need to drive to the store. Then, Netflix began streaming video. This format became the norm instead of the exception, and Netflix cemented streaming video as its primary viewing model.

When Netflix created original programming and released an entire series at one time (rather than following the traditional industry model of releasing one new episode per week), customers began consuming content in an unprecedented way called *binge watching*. The concept of watching programs whenever you want, wherever you want, and starting at the beginning of the series was one game changer. The other game changer was that Netflix figured out how to recommend content based on your user profile. The company was personalizing your experience.

This is just one example of how quickly society moves from a one-size-fits-all model to a more personalized approach. In fact, people born after 1981 (McCrindle, 2014) have completely different patterns of consuming content compared to their parents and grandparents (Content Science, 2016). Movies aren't the only disrupted medium. In 2006, record labels reported over $9 billion in CD sales revenue. By 2016, their sales had dropped 84 percent (Russell & Sisario, 2016). Why? Because of streaming music services like Napster, iTunes, Spotify, Pandora Internet Radio, and Amazon Music. Even the devices that we use to consume content have changed, evolving from televisions to portable DVD players, and from record players to Walkmans to CD players to MP3 players. Where are those devices now? They have been pushed aside in favor of tablets and pocket-sized phones. Growing up in a culture with unprecedented choices leads to students who take personalization for granted. Those born after 1981 want to see opportunities for voice and choice incorporated into their learning at school.

Infrastructure is important in terms of what and how people consume content (Wi-Fi, hot spots proliferation, and higher network speeds, for example), but we argue that it is the innate desire to personalize our experiences that really powers this shift. This innate desire to personalize everything, coupled with a world that makes it possible, drives many conversations. Here's why: although students are comfortable owning the information they consume in their personal lives, they have few opportunities to own anything in school. Want to take advanced Spanish? Sorry. That's not possible given your current schedule and current class offerings. Passionate about studying climate change or the life of Hemingway or computer programming? You'll have to wait. That's covered in another class or another grade level or another year. The truth is that there is a real disconnect between how we consume information and pursue our own passions and interests in and beyond the schoolhouse walls.

Defining Personalized Learning

Personalized learning means students choose their learning resources, design their learning experiences, and have flexibility over how to make their thinking visible. Personalization means specifically "enabling student voice and choice" during mastery (Abel, 2016). A student's interests and needs are foremost—not teacher-driven, rigid curriculum.

What's more, educators ask students during personalized learning to reflect on *how learning happens*. We must ask for their insights on further personalizing our classrooms. Failing to ask means failing to introduce personalized learning at scale. For the purpose of this book, we define *scale* as the intentional expansion of a desired combination of knowledge, dispositions, and skills. Structures and readiness indicators that scale learner voice and choice will positively impact more learners through a systemic shift within and between classroom and school communities.

Well-intentioned vendors and educational bureaucracies often inadequately define, infrequently apply, and dilute opportunities for learners to chart their own paths. Only after thoroughly defining learner voice and choice, as well as distinguishing personalized learning from other frameworks, do we present practical advice to K–12 teachers and district leaders.

Defining Learner Voice and Choice

Clarifying complicated concepts starts with accurately defining key terminology (Schmoker, 2004). We mean the following when we talk about learner voice and choice.

- A *learner* is anyone who engages in learning, regardless of age or role. Teachers are learners too, and authentic student voice and choice can't be empowered until teachers and administrators realize self-efficacy in their own voices and choices. For the adults, professional learning will shift to model the important aspects of voice and choice to support new learning. Everything in this book applies equally to teachers, administrators, and students. All are learners.

- *Voice* is a learner's passionate acquisition and sharing of new learning. Voice isn't necessarily audible. It represents ongoing external and internal dialogues in efforts to create conditions that empower deep learning through inquiry, collaboration, and mistake making. Understanding voice requires frequent practice, clear feedback, curiosity, and courage.

- Learners' decisions, which their individual and collective voices inform, qualify as *choice*. These decisions can be personal and limited to one individual or they can apply to groups of learners who share a common purpose. Voice sparks dialogue and choice signifies every action, small or large, that empowers exploration and creation. Ironically, as students are educated within a traditional school, standardization blunts their capacity for authentic choice (Robinson, 2012).

Students who can guide their own learning are invested. Invested students are engaged and higher achieving (Richmond, 2014). Students *and* teachers deserve this. Providing students with a place to voice their needs and interests, and a place for choice in the process, starts with teachers.

Distinguishing Personalized Learning From Other Frameworks

Many personalized learning definitions circle back and focus on teachers. As much as we believe in teachers as co-creators, many respected sources emphasize the teacher's role—not the student's—in personalizing learning (Bill and Melinda Gates Foundation, 2014). Until teachers and administrators recognize the real differences among personalized, differentiated, and individualized learning, efforts to truly personalize learning experiences will flounder. Personalization is learner centered; differentiation and individualized learning are teacher centered. Differentiation and individualization require the teacher to provide instruction and set learning goals. Differentiation and individualization build on seat time, as opposed to competency-based learning, which advances based on content mastery (Bray & McClaskey, 2014).

Personalized learning means learners do the following.

- Participate in designing their learning.
- Identify learning plan goals and benchmarks.
- Acquire the skills to select and use the appropriate resources.
- Build a network of peers, experts, and teachers to guide and support their learning.
- Demonstrate content mastery in a competency-based system.
- Become self-directed experts who monitor their own progress and reflect on learning.

This book will give teachers, site leaders, and district teams the tools and resources for personalizing learning and implementing student voice and choice in the classroom and beyond.

Using This Book

Depending on your focus, you might be interested in specific topics. Engage with each section in a personalized way. Chapter 1 explains how to help amplify student voice. Chapter 2 gives teachers tools for empowering student choice. Chapter 3 presents a framework that takes these outcomes to school and district scale. The two former chapters include TED Talks and TEDxYouth Talks presentations because they add the authentic context for why this work is important. We deliberately chose speeches that students gave, because students make it worth engaging in this work. In the epilogue we turn to these experts who share their stories and bring personalized learning to life.

We provide detailed readiness indicators, structures, and data that can support students, classroom educators, and district and site administrators and teams as they collaboratively build systems that promote voice and choice. *Structures* in this context are the resources and tools that help educators realize personalized learning. Readiness indicators correspond to the look-fors that leaders can identify as milestones that measure the impact of these resources and tools. The epilogue reiterates that teachers don't need a districtwide implementation plan to use student voice and choice in the classroom right now.

Chapter 1
Empowering Learner Voice

After seeing Afghan car-bombing victims during a news report, then middle schooler Erik Martin wanted to create a memorial observation for war victims. During his 2013 TEDxYouth speech, Martin clarifies how he created his own goals (TEDxYouth, 2013). By applying learning to a context that was meaningful to him—taking on a current real-world cause, setting goals, and finding solutions—Martin tried to authentically participate in and reflect on his learning.

He states, "Unfortunately, this is exactly the sort of thing that doesn't fit into our typical standardized school schedule, and my school couldn't really provide the framework to help [facilitate his goal]" (TEDxYouth, 2013). This occurred despite efforts by Martin and one of his most inspirational teachers. The failure was a result of a system that was not built to allow student voice as a part of learning, and that wasn't equipped to embrace failure as a way to deepen understanding.

In his speech, Martin ponders, "How can innovation occur in such settings" (TEDxYouth, 2013)? School should prepare students for the real world, but it lacks the perspective of the very people it's supposed to prepare. It fears failure and therefore doesn't allow for experimentation. To create a culture that amplifies student voice, we must develop systems in which students have plenty of opportunities at all levels to struggle with the prospect of failure. Martin explains, "In school we are not taught to overcome a challenge, we are taught to fear the prospect of failure" (TEDxYouth, 2013). The lack of such systems to foster and amplify student voice within a school's structures made it impossible for Martin to meet his goals. In the face of traditional education's failure, think about this: two-thirds of students define success as mastering their own personal learning goals (Project Tomorrow, 2012).

Student voice—knowing what they need in order to learn—empowers students to participate in the learning process. Reflect carefully and honestly at the opportunities you offer students to practice exercising their voice throughout their learning process. Opportunities for *metacognition* (thinking about their thinking) are key to students developing reflective mindsets as they understand their needs. A teacher modeling by thinking aloud is a great way to encourage metacognition (Fogarty, 1994). Reflecting on your classroom's structures can reveal opportunities.

Structures That Can Promote Learner Voice

Student voice encourages dialogue—between teacher and student, between student and student, and even within a student him- or herself (in the course of reflection). You can initiate and encourage that dialogue within your classroom's basic structures, including norms and expectations, assignments, questions, individual and group goals, student roles, and technology.

Norms and Expectations

Facilitating the development of classroom norms invites students to share their personal values in a central artifact that validates their contributions throughout the year. In the process, students and teachers are building culture for learner voice, blocking out space for reflecting on not only behaviors but their own learning. Some norms that classrooms create to support student voice are born out of the concept of psychological safety. In these classroom environments, students are encouraged to take risks without the fear of being embarrassed or rejected. Interpersonal trust is celebrated.

Step back. Allow students to lead with their own norms. That said, the teacher is by no means passive. Ensuring that students understand *why* and *how* they are doing this sets the tone for this activity. Educators who offer students time to create basic norms around collaboration, problem solving, time management, and even play, for example, provide valuable learner voice opportunities in a domain that is often defined by adults. By incorporating this level of student voice into day-to-day process and curriculum, educators stimulate the necessary practice that empowers learner choice in their interpretation of and reflection on these norms. Reinforcing the application of these norms during a particular project or academic year requires careful attention and guidance, especially if students aren't accustomed to living by their norms.

Personalizing Through Example

Molly Mohler (Mariemont Elementary School, California) invites her kindergarten students to create simple norms in the first week of the school year. Every Friday afternoon, they reflect on how they upheld their class norms as well as read and discuss a book that highlights the behaviors they have prioritized (personal communication, July 27, 2017).

Drew Baker (Henrico County Public Schools, Virginia) facilitates a process whereby each of his classes defines and upholds its respective constitutions as a means of understanding various governmental structures. Throughout the year, students compare their self-defined goals with constitutions that promote various forms of government, economy, and society. Over time, Drew's involvement in these dialogues evolved from facilitator to thoughtful observer, as students took on increasingly sophisticated levels of introspection and synthesis (personal communication, June 20, 2017).

Assignments

Educators who clearly define and reinforce assignments tend to produce more engaging learning activities for students, prompting more thoughtful responses. Inviting students to participate in this process is highly recommended. To participate, they must reflect first internally, and then externally, with you, on what works best for them as learners. Their voice will become clearer to them. Allowing students to complete Howard Gardner's (1983) multiple intelligence and learning styles assessment (www.miresearch.org/midas/midas-2) is one way to promote internal reflection. Their insights will reveal places where you can adjust existing policies and practices.

Consider whether assignments reflect some or all the characteristics in table 1.1. Not all assignments can have any of these characteristics. If a singular currency binds K–12 classrooms across virtually every conceivable demographic, it has to be readily accessible worksheets and multiple-choice tests. Why are we recognizing opportunity within this realm? Students and teachers can easily hack either worksheets or multiple-choice tests to accommodate student inquiry, reflection, and goal setting—crucial student voice components.

Questions

Questions allow students to be curious, voice what they want to learn, and share new learning. The first teacher to gain infamous status in the Western world was Socrates. While this educator's prominence was galvanized by his student Plato's writings, it is his instructional approach that remains relevant thousands of years later. Socrates rarely lectured, preferring an inquiry-based approach that forced his students to apply logic toward the creation of their own answers and questions. We reference this ancient Greek philosopher because it is impossible to empower student voice without understanding the nature of questions in our classrooms. Consider the following realities.

- **There is a dramatic disparity in the number of questions students and teachers generate:** Teachers formulate and ask the overwhelming majority of questions to students (Vogler, 2008). This gap produces an unchallenged veneer of the teacher as controller of knowledge and the student as passive recipient.

- **The types of questions teachers ask are disproportionately low level:** According to Kathleen Cotton's (2014) study, 60 percent of teachers' questions prompt recall or comprehension responses, which represent the lowest levels of Bloom's (1956) taxonomy.

- **Teachers hurl hundreds of questions at students a day:** Over the course of a school day, teachers ask between three

Table 1.1: Ideal Assignment Characteristics

Characteristic	Explanation	Example
Multiple pathways	Students can successfully demonstrate understanding through more than one format or medium or when completing a minimum number of problems from an assigned pool.	A high school physics teacher shares lecture videos, resources, and assignments for a unit on waves. Using a rotation model, students choose how to consume the content and complete the assignments. They use class time to secure help, collaborate in small groups, and prepare for the unit assessment.
Points of reflection	Students can share their epiphanies, questions, and connections with the outside world through an assignment that has built-in structures encouraging reflection.	A fourth-grade teacher facilitates a storytelling project that focuses on building student peer-review skills. Students incorporate peer review into three story revisions prior to sharing reflections on their process at a local independent bookstore.
Diverse audience	Students can offer quality contributions more frequently when they know their work will be displayed before peers or an audience beyond their teacher (Northwest Regional Educational Laboratory, 2000).	A middle school plans fall and spring exhibition nights to showcase student artifacts that align to the district vision for personalized learning. Among the most well-attended nights of the year, students host family and community members as they share and reflect on artifacts created to solve authentic problems within and beyond their school.
Real-world connection	Students can apply knowledge and skill to a simulation or to engage with events and people outside the classroom because assignments enhance participation and engagement (Northwest Regional Educational Laboratory, 2000).	An elementary and middle school partner with a nonprofit organization that hosts after-school internships facilitated by employees representing local businesses. These weekly sessions provide students real-world experience in applying soft skills and academic curriculum.

hundred to four hundred questions (Vogler, 2008). What's more, these questions are close ended, meaning that the answer for each question alludes to a singular fact or response.

In our work with educators, we find that documenting and then reflecting on how questions exist in classrooms via Bloom's (1956) taxonomy is one of the most powerful means of empowering deeper learner voice by helping students articulate various thinking orders and questions at various levels. At the same time, we recognize the irony of asking teachers to gather more data. We are talking about data that educators experience as deeply beneficial.

Being aware of wait time, or the quiet between a question and a student's answer, as well as encouraging students to create individual and group goals, also both amplify student voice.

Bloom's Taxonomy

At the outset of many aspiring teachers' first education methods course is Bloom's (1956) taxonomy. From that point, his taxonomy of learning domains—which culminates in higher-order-thinking questions—anchors much pedagogical, curriculum, and assessment planning. What happens when teachers share this taxonomy with students? They then possess the language with which to reflect and discuss their learning, leading to dialogue between and with students. That dialogue allows students to reflect not only on what they learn, but how. See *Raising the Rigor* (Depka, 2017) to read more about creating higher-order-thinking questions according to Bloom's taxonomy regardless of grade level.

To track the Bloom's taxonomy application in your classroom, invite one or two trusted colleagues to participate in the following activity. Take a piece of blank paper and draw a big triangle on it. Divide the triangle in half with a horizontal line through its midpoint. On the left outside of the triangle, write *Teacher*. On the right outside of the triangle, write *Student*. (Visit **go.SolutionTree.com/instruction** to download a free reproducible of this form.) Your colleague visits your classroom for twenty minutes during your instruction. Your colleague should place a tally mark below the dividing line every time you, the

Personalizing Through Example

Rachel Toy (Henrico County Public Schools, Virginia) ensures that any handout she uses in her middle school science classroom meets the needs of at least three of Gardner's (1983) multiple intelligences (personal communication, August 9, 2017). They include musical-rhythmic, visual-spatial, verbal-linguistic, logical-mathematical, bodily-kinesthetic, interpersonal, intrapersonal, and naturalistic. This threshold allows students to experiment with different problem-solving approaches and sparks rich opportunities for small- and large-group synthesis.

Natasha Rowell (Green Bay Area Public School District, Wisconsin) supports teachers as they facilitate literature circles to reinforce student connections among reading, critical thinking, and writing. Using a common, open-ended packet, students in small groups apply their reading roles, including a predictor, a connector, a summarizer, and a questioner (personal communication, October 2, 2017).

Assessment hacking comes in different forms as well. Mike Harris (Guy Phillips Middle School, North Carolina) places a symbol next to each of his test questions to signify what level of Bloom's (1956) taxonomy it aims to assess. For instance, he indicates lower-order-thinking questions that require only fact recall, mid-order-thinking questions that require using information in new situations, and higher-order-thinking questions that demand evaluation (Bloom, 1956). This visual cue helps him maintain a balanced array of question types. His students grow to recognize the characteristics of each type of question, prompting a more intentional approach to problem solving (personal communication, August 8, 2017).

Amanda Psarovarkas (Bayside Intermediate School, Texas) coaches colleagues at her middle school to provide students with practice using question stems that correspond to varying levels of inquiry. To review for an upcoming assessment, students create sample test items and answers using these stems and their knowledge of the course content. They then work in small groups to share their approaches to solving a wide range of problems, many of which appear on the student's assessment (personal communication, August 8, 2017).

Department chairs at Shawsheen Regional Technical High School outside Boston, Massachusetts, work with an instructional coach to translate aspects of their vocational education programs into core mathematics, science, language arts, and social studies curriculum frameworks. Their goal is to ensure that all students understand content. They facilitate this by requesting continual application as opposed to memorization (J. Cook, personal communication, June 16, 2017). Studying the protocols and learning objectives in many of the vocational programs helps core-content teachers replicate structures that empower additional student voice in their classrooms.

teacher, or a student asks a foundational question (recall or comprehension per Bloom's taxonomy). Every time he or she hears a higher-order-thinking question (which includes analysis, synthesis, evaluation, or creation; Bloom, 1956), your colleague should place a tally mark on the appropriate side of the triangle above the dividing line.

What do these data reveal? A baseline measure against which you can innovate. You get that baseline by deconstructing the types of questions each student (and you) asks. What subtle adjustments to your questions can you make to increase the proportion of student responses that show higher-order thinking? What easy lesson tweaks will provide students a chance to wrestle with and ask deeper questions?

Personalizing Through Example

Superintendent Eric Godfrey (Buckeye Union High School District, Arizona) observed a student-led Socratic seminar in Jed Hayes's high school English and philosophy class. He was so impressed with the results of their inquiry-driven approach that he invited two of the students to Socratically facilitate his next executive cabinet meeting (K. Klein, personal communication, September 11, 2015).

Teachers Theresa Fletcher and Debbie Porter (Winnfield Senior High School, Louisiana) spent an entire year collaboratively developing lessons and then videotaping key moments of their lessons so they could study how certain types of follow-up questions maximize student comprehension (T. Fletcher and D. Porter, personal communication, February 2, 2011).

Fourth-grade teacher Renita Street (Martinsville City Public Schools, Virginia) places four colored cups at each of her student tables. During the first month of the school year, she teaches her students question stems that clarify (red cup), summarize (yellow cup), predict (green cup), and connect (black cup). At regular intervals in her instruction, she pauses for a full minute to allow students a chance to generate their own questions and lift the appropriate cup in the air to identify the type of question they are prepared to ask (personal communication, December 1, 2011).

Wait Time

Wait time is simply the quiet moments between when a teacher asks a question and when a student fully responds to it (Rowe, 1972). Regularly incorporating wait time strategies and using just *three seconds* of wait time result in more diverse, higher-order-thinking responses (Cazden, 2001; Rowe, 1972; Stahl, 1994) and facilitate coherent responses and new meaning creation. What's more, the educators who *do not* consistently monitor wait time *also* answer their own questions at a higher frequency than average (Walsh & Sattes, 2011). This research offers educators a simple, powerful means by which to build student comfort and skill through the unpacking of questions that align with higher-order-thinking outcomes.

Draw a simple chart to investigate your own wait time. (Visit **go .SolutionTree.com/instruction** to download a free reproducible chart like the one in figure 1.1.) Draw three sliders on the page, one short, one medium, one long. Each slider represents wait times of less than one second, between one and two seconds, and more than two seconds. Below the sliders, write *Teacher-answered questions* (or *TAQ*). Invite a colleague to preview twenty minutes of your instruction, and ask him or her to mark a tally next to the appropriate category after each question asked. For example, assume you ask students a question. If you wait for two seconds before providing an answer, your colleague marks a tally beside *More than two seconds*.

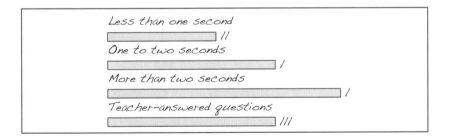

Figure 1.1: Chart your wait time.

*Visit **go.SolutionTree.com/instruction** for a free reproducible version of this figure.*

Experiment with the following techniques and phrases.

- **Lead time:** "In ten seconds, I'm going to ask a question. Prepare yourselves!"

- **Wait time context:** "Please take twenty seconds to reflect on your response prior to raising your hand" or "Please take twenty seconds to think before turning to a neighbor to share your thoughts."

- **Response diversity:** "I'm not going to call on anyone until I see ten hands in the air" or "Please go to the backchannel to share your answer."

Personalizing Through Example

Lluvonia Graham's (Clear Creek Independent School District, Texas) ninth- and tenth-grade students maintain their own blogs to help them explore ideas, refine select writings, and prepare for peer-led literary talks (personal communication, December 26, 2015).

Tenth-grade students in Teresa Davis's classroom record observations and questions on a digital Cornell notes form during Socratic dialogues. Occasionally, she provides them with the opportunity to contribute with a *backchannel*—a conversation that allows students to ask questions without interrupting the teacher or activities (Rogers, 2016)—such as TodaysMeet, and projects it at the front of class (personal communication, January 14, 2013).

Individual and Group Goals

A classroom culture that prioritizes and supports short- and medium-term *individual* and *group goals* provides students with opportunities to develop autonomy. That autonomy gives voice to what students learn and when they learn it. It makes sense to introduce goal setting and reflection into a classroom culture.

Talking to students about their goals outside of the typical context of classroom instruction can also lead to thoughtful dialogue. You can try the following suggestions when involving students in meaningful conversations about the education process.

Personalizing Through Example

Bill Rosene (Buckeye Union High School District, Arizona) uses an adaptive learning program that challenges students according to their current abilities. Bill teaches his students to clearly set and share daily and weekly learning goals, which he supports through small-group instruction. All students naturally apply the language of mathematics in their small groups as they collaborate to solve problems (personal communication, August 3, 2017).

High school faculty at Hidden Valley High School in Roanoke, Virginia, host exhibition nights each fall and spring. The entire community is invited to attend and watch students present their projects and ask questions for clarification and student reflection promotion. These occasions have become major events, which hundreds of family members, community and business leaders, and other educators attend. Students are the sole presenters (R. Stegall, personal communication, April 2, 2015).

- **Set up regular collaboration times with multiple students from different age groups around important, meaningful topics:** Creating a culture of collaboration with multiple student groups will support a more balanced student-teacher partnership. To maintain meaningful conversations, groups must meet regularly and allow students opportunities to offer their own topics.

- **Collect student feedback often and illustrate how their input directly correlates to school outcomes and processes:** You can, for example, ask students to participate in a visioning activity that charts the path for personalized learning in the district and then involve them in committees that operationalize the vision. If students realize they impact outcomes, they are more likely to take the time and provide more honest feedback (Toshalis & Nakkula, 2012).

- **Involve students in district- and school-based committees:** Collaboration might involve requests for proposal, strategic planning, and hiring committees. Student participation in these types of committees can lead educators to rethink aspects of the school's education systems.

Student Roles

Through various roles, teachers facilitate student discovery of their emerging voices via experimentation and study. A student's capacity to learn directly relates to the number and quality of opportunities to practice using his or her voice. Teachers can create specific roles that allow students to focus on a limited range of responsibilities and skills in order to provide students with regular exposure and feedback. This scaffolded practice has teachers assign roles to develop the practice and students taking responsibility over time.

What are some sample roles? They can be as simple as assuming the perspective of a historical character while conducting research in a social studies class. Some teachers create complex structures that distribute responsibilities to students throughout the entire academic year. At the outset of each year, high school mathematics teacher Colonel Allan Bean's boss system allows students to co-manage basic tasks—homework boss, supplies and materials boss, classroom rules boss, and so on (A. Bean, personal communication, May 19, 2010). He even employs a time boss, who monitors his lecture time and stops him if he strays beyond fifteen consecutive minutes of direct instruction. By sharing these responsibilities, he clearly defines roles for individuals in small-group projects, enhancing all participants' learning levels (Erickson, 2012).

Personalizing Through Example

Tim Towslee is an eleventh-grade English teacher (Glen Allen High School, Virginia) who lets his students choose a famous writer whose style they imitate to refine their written voice. From Chaucer to Hemingway and Poe to Dante, students are stepping into the shoes of other writers as a means of discovering their own identities as writers and thinkers. Students will develop fan clubs around voices of famous writers as a first step to empowering them to manage their own creative writing spaces over time (personal communication, October 11, 2012, and March 28, 2013).

Principal Charles Gregory (North Middle/High School, South Carolina) empowered a senior to serve as student principal on behalf of his peers. In this role, the student balanced his regular studies with a true full-time liaison job (A. Brennen, personal communication, May 31, 2016).

Technology

Blended learning combines technology with classroom learning to change the nature of pace, place, path, and time of learning. Doing so can help you identify functionality and technological tools worth incorporating into your learning activities. For example, most teachers use some form of learning management system to organize and share content with students, but these platforms provide little similarity to those that students have embraced in their personal lives. Even educational platforms that copy social media user interfaces lack the functionality that gets to the core of prioritizing student voice in the learning process, outcomes, and reflection. Students want to engage virtually in spaces that are visually appealing and allow flexible learning acquisition and processing, interaction with content, and collaboration with peers.

Try employing platforms that include portfolios so students can reflect on their own work and get feedback from peers and experts. This functionality allows students to set goals, monitor progress, embrace failure, and celebrate success. That give-and-take between users is the kind of external dialogue that helps users recognize what works for them when they're learning. This functionality also allows them to develop a collection of artifacts that document their learning—learning that isn't always evident or available on a traditional transcript. Chapter 2 (page 21) talks more about students choosing different ways to exhibit learning.

The blended learning community is full of tools and resources that can support student voice in the learning process and in school or district decisions. Write About (www.writeabout.com), Padlet (http://padlet.com), Google Cardboard (https://vr.google.com/cardboard) virtual reality design, and *Minecraft* (https://minecraft.net) allow multiple learning evidence opportunities. For example, running a backchannel on TodaysMeet (www.todaysmeet.com) or Twitter (www.twitter.com) can foster opportunities for voice in real time. (Visit **go.SolutionTree.com /instruction** to access live links to the websites mentioned in this book.)

Student Voice in Classroom and Schoolwide Decisions

Truly valued student voices are heard beyond classroom assignments. That means student voice should inform classroom, school, and even district decisions. Evaluate the quality of your school's student leadership groups with the following questions.

- Does our student leadership group invite new voices?

- How many students in our leadership group has the typical learning process disenfranchised?

- How and where does our student leadership group get the information it needs to represent the wider student body?

- At which points are the students in our leadership group brought into decision making?

- Do the students in our leadership group have a meaningful role among multiple school or district committees?

One Last Story on Learner Voice

Adam facilitated Arlington County Public Schools leaders, community members, school board officials, teachers, and students as they deeply discussed learning that meets students' needs and what that looks like in action. During this 2011 discussion, an exchange between a business owner and a student encapsulated why student voice is critical to designing a better vision for schools. The business owner said that the student was smart, and he shouldn't care if other students do well, since after graduation he would be competing with them. The student replied that he appreciated the compliment but that a community can survive only if everyone knows how to work together, solve problems, and support each other. That comment, much like those Erik Martin made during his TEDxYouth (2013) speech, reinforces why it makes sense to involve students in discussions about rethinking the system.

Start talking to students about school in a context that values what students have to say—for example, problem-finding activities about school and district issues that result in a forum where students present their solutions.

Chapter 2
Empowering Learner Choice

In her TED Talks speech, twelve-year-old Adora Svitak reminds us that "kids are not hampered by the same things that adults think about when deciding not to do something" (TED, 2010). She goes on to highlight the curiosity and need for choice that students have as they learn. Despite that, seminal education author Alfie Kohn (1993) says that "schooling is typically about doing things *to* children, not working *with* them." Svitak recognizes the lack of these opportunities in school, suggesting that a lack of choice is a question of trust. She asserts that adults simply don't believe that students are willing to accept more responsibility for their own learning. That fosters a dangerous culture of low expectations in schools. In Svitak's ideal world, which mirrors many students' ideals, adults know that as long as they receive support, they can trust students to make great choices about how they learn best and how to show what they learn.

Students exercising choice results in learning spaces where they feel invested and energized. Look a little closer and you discover that choice is important because it prevents students from getting burned out (Kohn, 1993). As Kohn (1993) asserts, "A lack of control over what one is doing" is what best predicts burnout.

Giving students a choice in both the context of the learning process and how to demonstrate mastery recognizes and respects their desire for customization. It doesn't take many conversations with students to understand there is a vast difference in the way students learn outside of school and the way they learn in school. For example, outside of school, students often use Google, YouTube, and Alexa from Amazon when they want or need to learn something. Inside school, they are asked to write notes from an authority and recite that information during a test. The majority of that difference is choice.

You can promote learner choice at school by modifying structures—creating opportunities for learning at different times and locations or letting them specify the tool or medium through which they show mastery. When students indicate with their understanding and practices that they are ready, you can begin incorporating student choice in class and schoolwide decisions. We'll wrap up this chapter with one last story on learner choice.

Structures That Can Promote Learner Choice

A decision reflects learner choice. Voice informs choice. The following sections describe ways teachers can give students more choice *right now*, including technology, free choice time, learning exhibition, midpoint decisions, content variation, life skills promotion, and conflict resolution.

Even though the following sections discuss foundational instructional practices, we urge even the most experienced and accomplished educators to reflect on how they apply these practices in their classrooms. Exploring simple, powerful adjustments in their pedagogy allows educators across departments and grade levels to empower student choice without expensive resources, sophisticated technology, or cutting-edge architecture.

Technology

Scale, the ability to ensure a best practice is employed throughout an organization, is one of the greatest barriers to providing students with choice. Removing this barrier requires understanding the problem and implementing the right tools. Technology, which constantly evolves, is often the key to scalable solutions when it comes to providing learners choice about how they obtain information. The simple truth is that digital tools for content consumption and creation can be invaluable resources for any teacher or school interested in incorporating more choice into the classroom.

Take content consumption, for example. Technology puts information into a format other than textbooks. Users create and consume hundreds of YouTube (www.youtube.com) videos, send hundreds of thousands of text messages, view billions of Snapchat (www.snapchat.com) videos, and translate tens of millions of words on Google (Aslam, 2017; Dieker, 2016). A teacher needn't provide students with information that they then consume. Instead, teachers must help students make educated choices about the sources they are already consuming.

Choice over content comes with the responsibility of evaluating each individual source for bias, inaccuracy, and intentional misinformation. Many students are poorly prepared to evaluate accurately. Need proof? The results of a year-long Stanford University study conclude that middle school, high school, and college students "struggled to distinguish ads from articles, neutral sources from biased ones and fake accounts from real ones" (as cited in Domonoske, 2016). With this phenomenon increasing in society for all citizens, we need to ensure that digital literacy becomes a focus in every literacy plan.

Technology also allows students to show mastery in multiple ways. However, at no other time in history has the impact of information created and shared on the internet had such learner-empowering potential. With so many resources available, demonstrating mastery can become a genuine choice individual students make within your classroom.

Teachers and administrators must decide the following about the role technology can play in providing students with choices.

- **How students will access content:** Try discussion boards, fan fiction sites, YouTube videos and comments, and so on.

- **How students will access the digital tools needed to make their thinking visible:** Access models can vary based on available resources, including 1:1, station rotation models, labs, and bring your own device (BYOD). Digital tool organization within these models can occur via free resources such as G-Suite for Education (https://edu .google.com/products/productivity-tools) or Symbaloo (www.symbaloo.com) or paid services in learning management or student information systems.

- **How teachers will provide a scaffolded learning process for digital citizenship, including digital literacy:** Resources such as Google's Be Internet Awesome (https://beinternetawesome.withgoogle.com/resources) or Common Sense Media's digital citizenship modules (www.commonsense.org/education/digital-citizenship) provide support.

- **The policy for using digital tools that share data:** Discussing potentially adopted digital tools and data privacy requirements is critical. The Family Educational Rights and Privacy Act (1974) as well as the Children's Online Privacy Protection Act (1998) outline the data-sharing laws. In need of some guiding questions to get the conversation started? Connect Safely (www.connectsafely.org/eduprivacy) provides guiding questions during policy development.

- **When and how students will use technology in the learning process:** Technology should not lead design, but allow students to choose how they acquire and interact with information. For example, instead of having all students read an article to gain background knowledge on a topic, consider letting students choose how they want to acquire new information from resources text, video, simulation, or even a Skype session or Google Hangout with an expert.

- **How teachers can use technology to decide what content they consume and create in their professional learning:** Ideally, teachers and students do not log in to different systems but instead search across multiple content providers, open-source (free) materials, and teacher-created resources. That ease promotes choice and voice.

Consider encouraging students to make a movie to demonstrate concept mastery instead of presenting them with a written assessment. When making movies, students can choose from dozens of technologies.

- **Apps and software:** PowerDirector Mobile Video Editor (2017; http://bit.ly/2rsxU5s) and FiLMiC Pro (www.filmicpro.com)

- **Formats:** Microsoft or QuickTime multimedia container

- **Storage warehouses:** YouTube and Vimeo (https://vimeo.com)

- **Ways to share their final products:** Lino (http://en.linoit .com) and Padlet (www.padlet.com)

Teachers needn't explain the hows behind video production. Instead, you ask questions to help students make the best decisions given the learning situation's content and context.

- Does the content students are learning lend itself best to a traditional video? Suggest WeVideo (www.wevideo.com).

- Would animated characters add interest or intrigue to the message that students are trying to share? Try GoAnimate (https://goanimate.com).

To facilitate technology's use around student choice, teachers define and integrate skills with limited technology and time. They also define and manage blended learning (offline and online, in- and outside the classroom) opportunities.

Defining and Integrating Skills and Dispositions Within Technology

Carefully defining and integrating skills and dispositions—inherent qualities and mindsets that support learner inquiry—like critical thinking, communication, collaboration, creativity, citizenship, and social-emotional learning are non-negotiable in a personalized learning classroom. They are essential to successful learning. Understanding a personalized learning classroom's benefits and limitations is an equally important process to consider. While these two areas are included in the low-tech section of our discussion, the recommendations we outline and practices we share are useful to educators and students who attend schools that boast new or established one-to-one device capacity.

The transition from a traditional direct instruction model to one that welcomes and nurtures learner choice is too wide a gap for the simple inclusion of technology to bridge. As you navigate your way from traditional, textbook-based instruction to leveraging a wider, eclectic range of web-based resources, apps, and learning management systems, it is important to adopt a simplified language around what these skills can look like in their classrooms. Resources like the Substitution Augmentation Modification and Redefinition (SAMR) model (Puentedura, 2013) and technological pedagogical and content knowledge (TPCK or TPACK) framework (Mishra & Koehler, 2006) are great places to start. (Visit **go.SolutionTree.com/instruction** for live links that offer information about the model and framework.) They offer visual metaphors for what learning can look like at varying levels of technology integration.

These resources are limited, however, because they don't explore in detail how higher-order-thinking skills integrate within their curricula and assessment frameworks. A scaffolded, responsive professional learning sequence is critical to achieving this level of comfort and understanding and may include activities like ongoing collaboration with an outside or district coach, visiting and reflecting on practices demonstrated in model classrooms, and action research. These structures are responsive because educators have authentic voice for setting learning goals and collecting data that inform areas of study that are relevant to their students.

Collaborative planning, coaching, and sustained training on how soft skills can live harmoniously with fast-paced school days are fundamentally important. We observe an increasing number of districts and schools transitioning to diversified offerings of job-embedded and blended opportunities for application-based learning. Michele Staley and her teacher leadership team at Clear Brook High School incorporated a program that offers each educator an opportunity to frame independent learning goals, secure required resources, and share their findings with their colleagues throughout the year (M. Staley, personal communication, February 3, 2016).

Defining and Managing Blended Learning Opportunities

In 2007, educators Jon Bergmann and Aaron Sams came up with a simple question: What would happen if we used technology to allow educators to record and share their lectures with students? At that time, YouTube was gaining significant momentum as the preeminent solution for video sharing and more students had access to laptop computers (Noonoo, 2012). These educators aspired to seize this momentum to experiment with *flipping* classrooms, so that students were exposed to knowledge presentation for homework and were then ready to work with their peers and teachers on higher-order-thinking tasks in the classroom. Thousands of educators began experimenting with the flipped classroom. A number of pervasive problems arose in the midst of this rapid expansion.

- Students who didn't do their homework prior to flipped classes didn't magically start doing their homework afterward.

- Teachers who were uninspiring speakers didn't transform into captivating lecturers.

- Equity was a major issue because not all students had resources at home for this technology-dependent commitment.

This is not an indictment of flipped classrooms (which we consider an appropriate strategy but by no means a 3-D learning model) but an example of how technology pushed the traditional boundaries of time and space as they relate to school. Students were no longer anchored to a particular time of day and location when accessing information from their teachers. In this sense, learners discovered for the first time that technology allowed them to blend their learning, and an educator who is aware of the resources and platforms conducive to blended learning has massive potential for curriculum adaptations that empower learner choice.

The variety within the model often surprises educators who are new to the concept of blended learning. The Clayton Christensen Institute (n.d.; www.christenseninstitute.org) summarizes the various types of blended learning (such as station, lab, or individual rotation) that provide practical frameworks for integrating curriculum and technology while empowering learner choice.

Personalizing Through Example

David Finley (Redlands eAcademy, California) is principal at an alternative school that leverages blended learning to support students who haven't realized success in conventional classrooms. By transitioning courses to a learning management system, teachers and students alike can set goals, collaborate, and reflect on progress in their preferred spaces and paths, at their preferred paces (personal communication, January 11, 2015).

A Chicago-area high school teacher invites his students to prepare for an upcoming quiz using the technology available within and beyond their classroom. On his whiteboard, he writes down the various mathematics concepts and question types that he will assess. In groups of three, students choose a concept and develop a sample problem; they use a student device to record a brief video of their ability to successfully solve the problem at least two different ways. Students post their videos on Canvas (www.canvaslms.com), a digital learning platform that allows students to preview one another's work. Students also use these resources throughout the course (D. Richard, personal communication, September 17, 2015).

Free Choice Time

Set aside a daily or weekly time when students choose what they work on. Options include doing homework, working with a group on a project, creating art, visiting a makerspace to design and build, or writing. The goal isn't to get a specific product out of students during this time. It's to give students ownership over some of the time that they spend at school.

Learning Exhibition

Let students choose how they show their learning at the end of a unit. Move away from a defined product and give students the freedom to choose an artifact that best shows what they know, including videos, presentations, scripts, cartoons, and full museums. Allowing students to select both the tool and format for a final demonstration, instead of requiring everyone to complete the same assignment and present to the entire class, sends the message that learning can be creative and self-directed.

Midpoint Decisions

Give students choice over the flow of their learning. At the beginning of the unit, share data about what students know and don't know. Discuss how they should work to obtain new information. Simple formative tools and graphic organizers (Stiggins, 2008) promote natural, efficient processes for securing student-friendly data that allow for practice. Explain that mastery by the end of the unit is the expectation for every learner, but that students can suggest their own paths through the required content.

Content Variation

Give students access to a wide variety of content types—textbooks, open-source online content, simulations, videos, expert interviews—and let them choose which resources to learn from. The following resources are a starting point.

- **Open Educational Resource Commons** (www.oercommons.org) is a curated digital library and network of open resources coupled with the ability for educators to share and get feedback on their creations, which supports a variety of learning experiences and modalities.

- **Histography** (http://histography.io) is an interactive time line that spans fourteen billion years of historical events. Teachers can consider ways to engage students with information organized this way and provide peer and student-teacher collaboration.

- **TED-Ed** (http://ed.ted.com) is a youth and education initiative that offers curated content. Teachers can build lessons around original TED-Ed, TED Talks, or YouTube videos, which provide perspectives from people outside students' communities.

- **Wild-Touch's Ice & Sky history of climate change** (http://education.iceandsky.com) showcases various content types to help build a deeper understanding of climate change through a variety of perspectives. This interactive

documentary offers collaborative conversation and
questioning simulations.

- **DIY Gamer Kit** (2017; http://bit.ly/2rtRONY) helps
create a hands-on learning experience coupled with content
understanding, which lets students transcend their learning
in both physical and digital environments.

- **Student 21** (http://blogs.henrico.k12.va.us/student21)
shares Henrico County Public Schools' curated resources
from student, teacher, and leaders to inspire projects.

Life Skills Promotion

Separate the outcomes students must learn for a test from the skills
(like critical thinking, problem solving, and metacognition) and dispositions (like agency, adaptability, and leadership) that students need
to succeed in life. Students require chances to develop these skills and
dispositions and apply these outcomes in an authentic context. This
allows choice-driven *playlists* (a structure for organizing and accessing
resources to drive mastery) for knowledge-based learning and more
structured activities for outcomes that require complex thinking skills
and dispositions.

Conflict Resolution

Hold class meetings to deal with conflict resolution. Model how choice
plays a role in resolving student conflicts, where empathy and honesty
are key components of successful learner-led programs. Quaker Friends
Schools, including Carolina Friends School (Pendergrast, Layman,
Butchart, & Moore-Mott, 2012) and the Friends School at Minnesota
(http://bit.ly/2x5tEZy), have established very clear overviews of their
approach to building student autonomy in this area.

Student Choice in Classroom and Schoolwide Decisions

As you move from individual classrooms to the infinitely messier
and anxiety-inducing empowerment of learner choice across an entire

school, your greatest challenge will be maintaining teacher choice. That is the case because between the types and volume of the various state or provincial and federal standards frameworks, textbook content, and mind-bending benchmark assessments, we must state the obvious: learner choice is often at odds with the existing culture in many schools. Despite that, there are schools—large and small, rural and urban, public and charter, conventional and progressive—engaging in the difficult work required to move beyond these challenges, building learner choice into an entire school's everyday reality. How are these communities rethinking lesson planning, replacing directives with protocols, and balancing formative and summative assessments? While we present this information, we will maintain a practical focus on what faculty and staff at one school can accomplish over time. With focus and clarity, refining a school's culture to accommodate meaningful, interconnected learner choice is a practical, achievable goal.

Start by involving students in conversations around classroom rules and procedures and ask what steps should occur when a student doesn't follow those rules. These conversations are manageable because learners, teachers, and administrators have lots of experience with classroom rules and procedures. Classroom discussions and decisions will be informed, efficient, and likely to succeed.

It is essential, however, to involve students in deeper conversations about how daily learning happens and what tools and processes they will utilize to accomplish important work. Convincing students to accept responsibility for learning can only occur once they realize that you value their input on important issues like what content to study and the best ways to demonstrate mastery, which are issues that teachers have long controlled. Doing so ensures that you reach a wide range of learners—something that doesn't always happen when student choice is limited to superintendent or principal advisory councils that include a handful of students who have very little authority over big decisions that support personalized learning.

Try these ideas when involving students in the important decisions at your school.

- **Involve students in any committees or requests for proposals for tools or content that will impact learning:** Students should have a say in developing adoption rubrics and be voting members of the selection committee. This will provide decision-making ability in what tools students choose to support learning and how they use those tools.

- **Highlight products around the school that demonstrate and celebrate student choice:** During every staff meeting, call attention to student products and teacher learning activities that highlight choice. Designate an exhibition area in the building for artifacts that highlight learning choices.

- **Meet biweekly with students in forums you, and later students, facilitate to discuss learning:** During this time, provide students opportunities to choose the topics for discussion and let them share—without adult intervention. Over time, shift the facilitation of these conversations to your students. Let teachers watch, listen, and ask questions. The forums only work if students participate in solving problems.

One Last Story on Learner Choice

Adam and Amos worked with a school district to provide professional development to teachers around the concept of personalized learning. After a brief introduction to the core concepts, they decided to give participants a choice: learn more through a lecture, participate through a facilitated discussion, or watch videos and receive guided questions. Not surprisingly, Adam and Amos ended up with three fairly even groups. After twenty minutes, they asked teachers to work in trios; each trio included one member who had attended the lecture, one member who chose the facilitated discussion, and one member who had explored the video collection. Each group was charged with creating an artifact that would share its definition of personalized learning. The result was highly engaged learners who applied their own chosen experiences. For teachers to embrace choice as an important element of meaningful learning experiences, they have to experience it firsthand.

Education researcher and school-improvement advocate Phillip C. Schlechty (2002) may have said it best: "Schools cannot be made great by great teacher performances. They will only be made great by great student performances" (p. xiv). Great student performances begin and end with students who are empowered to choose the content that they consume and create. A culture of choice grows if teachers are encouraged to take instructional risks and gather student feedback when evaluating the changes they are making. If that kind of thinking doesn't seem rational, then return to Adora Svitak's TED Talks presentation. "Maybe irrational thinking is what the world needs" (TED, 2010).

Chapter 3
Empowering Learner Voice and Choice at Scale

Many school districts are currently engaged in a process to introduce and reinforce a new vision and mission for deeper voice and choice for all learners. Some districts position an upcoming technology initiative as a catalyst, while others choose an approach more closely aligned to progressive pedagogy, curriculum, or assessment (like personalized learning, project-based learning, or competency-based assessments). Regardless of what drives the change, district leadership—to whom we direct this chapter—must develop and facilitate a multiyear plan to produce a gradual, measured, and assertive shift from the existing traditional learning model to one that promotes deep learner voice and choice. States and provinces nurture innovation when they increase policy flexibility, provide technical assistance, support peer networks, and seek feedback on the changes (Sturgis & Patrick, 2010).

A district's effort to inform, empower, and challenge all stakeholders must transcend a conventional initiative's launch or public relations campaign's limitations. Scaffolded messaging, tangible exemplars, and just-in-time supports for students and staff drive ongoing community outreach, job-embedded professional development, and sustained innovation. In fact, it is crucial that states and provinces work with "districts and schools if they are to effectively expand competency-based practices and pathways" (Sturgis & Patrick, 2010, p. 15).

The readiness indicators and corresponding supports we offer in this chapter for the aforementioned stakeholder groups are grounded in best practices that Learning Forward's (n.d.) standards for professional learning (https://learningforward.org/standards), the International Society for Technology in Education (n.d.) standards for administrators (http://bit.ly/2qPRuG3), and Hewlett Foundation's (n.d.) vision and mission for deeper learning (www.hewlett.org/strategy/deeper-learning) validate. Furthermore, our hard-earned implementation experience forges these recommendations in different K–12 school districts. We encourage district-leadership teams to use the readiness indicators and support recommendations we provide to inform visioning, implementation planning, and budgeting efforts.

This chapter clarifies for district leaders the student, classroom educator, school site administrative team, and their own district administrator roles in empowering learner voice and choice beyond the classroom.

The Student Role

Any district that aspires to engage deep learner voice and choice beyond the scale of a few classrooms must clearly and bravely acknowledge its solitary outcome: to realign its deepest, most entrenched structures in a fashion that inspires self-actualization on behalf of each of its students. No district can accomplish this outcome without starting and ending with empathy for what voice and choice for all students look like at scale.

While clarifying and empathizing with student voice and choice at this level may seem a daunting prospect, many school systems succeed, including Hall County (Georgia) and Summit Schools (California; C. Emily, personal communication, April 29, 2011; V. Gamez, personal communication, May 30, 2017). Leadership teams and their school boards—which must remain active, committed partners throughout this transformation process—that aspire to this level of leadership identify exactly what learner voice and choice look like for students representing all demographics. By empowering district administrators, site leadership teams, and classroom educators with high-quality professional learning as well as well-articulated, transparent, and realizable goals, Hall County and Summit Schools are providing the tools that allow districts to build leadership capacity over a multiyear time line. Establishing common language is an extension of a collaboratively developed vision and mission. That common language, in fact, predicts sustainable, scaled educational change over time (Schooling, Toth, & Marzano, 2013). To this end, carefully define tangible, clear habits of mind; identify skills and knowledge that students will learn, reinforce, and eventually master; and align efforts with carefully communicated and supported district structures.

The readiness indicators in figure 3.1 (page 38) provide district executive teams with milestones and tangible look-fors, or readiness indicators, that can inform long-term planning efforts. The three tiers of readiness supports identify communication structures, professional learning priorities, and data that can inform real-time progress. Translating these outcomes into student-friendly language rubrics is a critical component to building student autonomy around these readiness indicators. A catalyst for this success is ongoing professional learning for administrators and principals on formative assessment pedagogy that incorporates goal-setting reflection and peer review into classroom procedures and curriculum planning. In Evergreen Public Schools (Washington), all curriculum specialists, content coaches, and administrators participate in scaffolded professional learning to apply common formative assessment strategies and protocols in their support of classroom educators (C. McMurray, personal communication, October 15, 2015).

Many aforementioned indicators and supports may seem self-evident. Any district-led efforts to establish and sustain learner voice and choice are indisputably linked to the extent to which the district executive team prioritizes student-centered development at the outset of such an initiative. In later implementation phases, when learner voice and choice are operating within personalized learning, students who are engaged as meaningful collaborators and apply skills refined among their peers from the outset provide the necessary capacity to achieve self-efficacy for all students (Bray & McClaskey, 2016).

Readiness indicators: To what extent can students measurably understand, practice, and reinforce opportunities that enhance voice and choice? What practical and apparent look-fors correlate with increasing complexity levels in these regards?

Emerging Readiness Indicators	Moderate Readiness Indicators	High Readiness Indicators
• Lack of ongoing professional development and clear common language restricts district elementary and secondary educators from promoting student voice and choice. At the classroom level, limited professional development and unclear curriculum exemplars create pockets of excellence in student access to voice and choice.	• Elementary student experience with learner voice and choice goes beyond app-driven exploration, remediation, and creativity. Students engage in purposeful, open-ended opportunities to develop higher-order-thinking skills through the initial years of district implementation.	• Elementary student experience with learner voice and choice is diverse, ubiquitous, authentic, and often self-driven. Students are comfortable with open-ended challenges and use a range of tools to personalize their learning as individuals and within groups.
• Students may experience opportunities to leverage technology for enhanced voice and choice, but this occurs sporadically and at varying quality levels. Most students are unaware of the terms *voice* and *choice* and how they connect to their learning.	• Secondary student experience with learner voice and choice leverages the foundation that elementary and middle grades establish. Collaboration, research, and creativity via a range of technology tools and an optional learning management system are emerging.	• Secondary student experience with learner voice and choice is fully realized. Collaboration, critical thinking, research, and creativity via a range of technology tools and an established learning management system are evident at target levels. All students deftly employ choice, goal setting, and formative feedback.
• Survey data demonstrate low levels of perceived student choice, goal setting, formative feedback, and open-ended technology use.	• Students at all grades supplement their face-to-face learning with an increasing array of blended and personalized options, both independently and via district curriculum and assessment frameworks.	• Students realize blended learning in efficient and unorthodox ways, such as enhancing learning within a competency-based grading structure or global massive open online courses.
	• Survey data demonstrate moderate levels of perceived student choice, goal setting, formative feedback, and open-ended technology use.	• Survey data demonstrate self-actualized levels of student choice, goal setting, formative feedback, and open-ended technology use.

Readiness supports: What training, practice, and ongoing dialogue with students are necessary to sustain opportunities for voice and choice with increased frequency and depth?

Emerging Readiness Supports	Moderate Readiness Supports	High Readiness Supports
• **Communications:** The district and its schools focus on promoting concepts of student voice and choice in student-friendly media campaign. District executive team enables student leadership cohorts (SLCs) at participating schools; successful applicants receive training to understand fundamentals of district voice and choice initiative. District executive team gathers a wide range of student response data outlining epistemological beliefs as a baseline measure to eventually realize vision and mission for learner voice and choice. • **Knowledge and skills development:** Students complete age-appropriate curriculum modules that promote vocabulary, skills, and dispositions that the district common language documents outline. Students who apply for the SLC positions will receive summer training. District executive team collects and analyzes student perceptions on voice and choice and applies these data toward creating sample lessons, units, and assessments for pilot implementation.	• **Communications:** Vocabulary, skills, and mindsets the district common language document outlines are visibly identified in student-based case studies at schools participating in the learner voice and choice initiative. All host schools have well-established SLCs, which bolster efficient meeting protocols and an expanding pool of online resources. A virtual platform captures district collection of student epistemological beliefs with increased frequency. • **Knowledge and skills development:** Students learn from SLC and each other as they continually improve their critical thinking, communication, collaboration, and creativity skills (four Cs; Partnership for 21st Century Learning, n.d.). SLC supports site-based leadership teams and classroom teachers with increased frequency and depth. Students interact with the virtual platform at or beyond a threshold level of frequency and engage in beginning phases of autonomous learning personalization.	• **Communications:** The district showcases student interviews and work samples as innovative, self-regulated exemplars of the district learner voice and choice initiative and vision for personalized learning. The district measurably identifies vocabulary, skills, and mindsets in common language document across all elementary and secondary classrooms. The district executive team promotes a wide range of learning opportunities for students that transcend traditional model and align with district vision for personalized learning. • **Knowledge and skills development:** The learning sessions that students create and facilitate populate a large proportion of technology-based training sessions for students. All students communicate and reflect on their learning using terminology in the district common language document. Students leverage an established personalized learning platform when appropriate.

Figure 3.1: Student readiness indicators and supports.

continued →

- **Feedback mechanisms:** Students respond to age-appropriate modules that they complete during homeroom, study block site-based sessions, and through optional virtual platforms. The district collects student certification rates for SLC positions. Student epistemological beliefs collected as a baseline measure for perceived voice, choice, and access in their learning.

- **Feedback mechanisms:** The district executive team analyzes change in student artifacts as it relates to the four Cs and district common language document; SLC meeting protocols at participating schools; and epistemological belief data gathered through virtual learning platform across a wide range of subject areas and grade levels.

- **Feedback mechanisms:** The district executive team continues analyzing change in student artifacts as it relates to four Cs and district common language document, consistently applying SLC meeting protocols across all schools. The district gathers epistemological belief data through personalized learning platforms. The team ensures that students lead active, purposeful roles in school and district-defined leadership roles.

Source: © 2014 by Advanced Learning Partnerships.

The Classroom Educator Role

Concurrent to developing student indicators and supports, district administrators must balance communications and resources to classroom educators in a fashion that models learner voice and choice. Simply put, students cannot realize self-efficacy without engaged classroom educators who define, apply, and continually refine their own professional self-efficacy skills and dispositions (The National Board for Professional Teaching Standards, 2016).

Our experience teaches that the most practical way for district administrative teams to accomplish professional self-efficacy is to dramatically redefine the outcomes, structures, and data that drive existing traditional professional development and evaluation programs. Three of the most important catalysts that provide classroom educators and students with enhanced voice and choice follow.

1. Education chats, or *edchats*, through various social media platforms such as Twitter

2. The shift to job-embedded professional learning (JEPL)

3. The professional learning community process (DuFour, DuFour, Eaker, Many, & Mattos, 2016)

Finally, our reference to *model classrooms*—hosting classrooms where educators engage in advanced professional learning specialized in implementing best practices that foster learner voice and choice—acknowledges the importance of activating local laboratory classrooms where educators, coaches, and specialists can see the district vision within their own communities.

The readiness indicators in figure 3.2 (page 42) provide educators with milestones and tangible look-fors that can inform long-term planning efforts. The three tiers of readiness supports identify communication structures, professional learning priorities, and data that can align to inform real-time progress.

Successfully transforming traditional district professional learning and evaluation programs to structures that prioritize educator voice and choice typically takes between two and five years, based on our

Readiness indicators: To what extent are classroom educators measurably able to define and facilitate opportunities for learner voice and choice? What practical and apparent look-fors correlate with increasing complexity levels in these regards?

Emerging Readiness Indicators	Moderate Readiness Indicators	High Readiness Indicators
• Classroom teachers are largely unaware of differentiated, individualized, and personalized learning models' characteristics in their lessons.	• Classroom teachers and coaches employ common protocols to refine and reflect on sample differentiated, individualized, and personalized lessons.	• Classroom teachers and coaches make informed, real-time decisions that broker authentic opportunities for learner voice and choice as well as personalized learning.
• Classroom teachers are largely unaware of the best practices associated with the development of a learner voice and choice culture and associated classroom management techniques.	• Classroom teachers and coaches work alongside students and parents to establish a practical, transparent learning environment that fosters learner voice and choice. Technology affords students enhanced access and choice.	• Teachers weave tangible outcomes aligned to learner voice and choice authentically throughout each school's culture. Classroom educators perceive learner voice and choice as worthwhile; ubiquitous access and informed choice are evident in everyday learning.
• Classroom teachers are largely unaware of technology's deep capabilities in fostering learner voice and choice. Technology either intimidates them, or they use it within the context of a direct instructive learning model.	• Classroom teachers and administrators are aware of the district personalized learning platform's functionality. They can facilitate and reflect on specific lessons with support from a coach or via established protocols.	• Classroom teachers and administrators access the personalized learning platform at multiple points each day. They leverage the tool to personalize curriculum and assessment in accordance with district targets leading learner voice and choice.
• Classroom educators are largely uncomfortable with the notion of JEPL. They express high anxiety when working with a coach, and cite a lack of time as the predominant reason for not participating.	• Model classroom educators, coaches, and administrators engage in JEPL. They invite interested colleagues to participate through model classroom visits and facilitated reflections with coaches.	• Collaborative model classroom teachers create well-established, vibrant hubs for professional learning. They are open to colleagues visiting

Readiness supports: What structures, resources, and data are necessary to support classroom educators as they facilitate deeper and more frequent opportunities for learner voice and choice?

Emerging Readiness Supports	Moderate Readiness Supports	High Readiness Supports
• **Communications:** The district applies branding such as logo, mascot, tagline, and hashtags to professional development communications to teachers. It clarifies and communicates a common language document to clarify and promote key terminology, dispositions, and skills. The district invites teachers to submit applications to serve as model classroom teachers in support of deployment. These teachers participate in coaching-based professional development and eventually host visits from colleagues in accordance to predefined protocols.	• **Communications:** The district applies branding to all student, teacher, and parent communications that outline learner voice and choice, four Cs, and digital citizenship. Professional development defines differentiated, individualized, and personalized learning descriptors through the district voice and choice model. The district develops, procures, and organizes high-quality materials for use in diverse professional development offerings. It promotes model classrooms as innovation centers hosted by local educators.	• **Communications:** The district branding expands to include case studies of innovative schools, community partnerships, and success stories of recent district graduates. Student work samples are shared as artifacts of the district vision and mission around learner voice and choice and personalized learning. The district highlights model classrooms as critical catalysts for learning, collaboration, and success.
		and learning from their emerging practice in alignment with predefined protocols. Teachers and coaches leverage both their local model classroom and the personalized learning platform to access an increasingly personalized professional learning portfolio.

Figure 3.2: Classroom educator readiness indicators and supports.

continued ↓

- **Knowledge and skills development:** Large-group and small-group professional development for teachers and administrators, as well as JEPL for curriculum specialists and department chairs, are established to clarify differentiation, individualization, and personalization. District offers personalized learning partner supports for spring and summer institutes on learner voice and choice, best practices for technology integration, and common language document. The district selects model classroom teachers, and the teachers have on-boarding via spring coaching and summer institutes.

- **Feedback mechanisms:** The district gathers stakeholder response regarding traditional and untraditional promotions. Inter-rater reliability around the application of the common language document increases. District professional development produces highly prepared, mobilized teachers in initiative pilot schools and model classrooms.

- **Knowledge and skills development:** Personalized learning training is available to educators in multiple formats. District and vendor coaching are available for model classroom teachers and expanding range of spring, summer, and fall institutes on digital citizenship, four Cs, learning management system, and common language document. The district facilitates three-week virtual courses for district educators for continuing education credit. An expanding cohort of model classroom teachers participates.

- **Feedback mechanisms:** The district gathers stakeholder response regarding traditional and untraditional promotions. Expanding cohorts of model classroom teachers partner with district specialists to lead a wide range of faculty professional development. The district gathers teacher feedback on virtual course participation.

- **Knowledge and skills development:** An ever-expanding cohort of students and educators is creating learning content based on community need. District teachers, specialists, and site educators are creating learning content based on community need. District teachers, specialists, and site leaders model best practices in model classrooms across all school sites. Teachers have a full, consistent range of professional learning options: large group, workshop, JEPL, and virtual. Intermediate and advanced training drives deep personalized learning platform integration.

- **Feedback mechanisms:** The district gathers stakeholder response to traditional and untraditional promotions. Personalized learning platform competency-based data describe adult and student learning growth. Coaches, administrators, and model classroom visiting teachers provide rich, multifaceted reflection.

Source: © 2014 by Advanced Learning Partnerships.

work with districts. Luckily, teacher-evaluation systems, aligned to the Performance Assessment of Competency Education in New Hampshire, are being implemented and reinforce realignment in rural, urban, and suburban school districts (New Hampshire Department of Education, 2016; Patrick, Worthen, Truong, & Frost, 2017). District teams already engaged in this professional capacity development may find including the aforementioned structures, resources, and data compatible with current efforts. Regardless of implementation scale or fidelity, many districts benefit from partnering with a reputable professional development organization (such as a regional center, college of education, or a private company). This is especially true during the transition to JEPL in the implementation's first few years.

The School Site Administration Team Role

While we maintain that the student role in scaled, sustained learner voice and choice is paramount, the critical role that site administrative teams play is a close second. Even more than classroom educators, the buy-in, authorship, and innovation that school principals and their support teams demonstrate are critical drivers for systemic school and district change. Learner voice and choice simply cannot scale and build enough momentum to transform the majority of classrooms, without the uninterrupted support of site-based leadership teams.

The need for this support is obvious but important to acknowledge. The evaluative roles that principals and assistant principals play conditions teacher response to local and district-defined priorities and milestones. This includes our focus on standardized tests and Carnegie units. If people in evaluative roles prioritize learner choice and voice, educators will do what they can to adjust practices. Done without clear, collaborative dialogue and adequate supports, however, educators and site administrators alike will respond in accordance to a perceived mandate, resulting in oversimplified practices, dog-and-pony shows on observation days, a noticeable drop in morale, and irreparable damage to district-communicated learner voice and choice as well as personalized learning initiatives (Elmore, 2000).

However, district leadership teams *can* adopt an intentional, gradual approach to supporting site administration teams through the transition from traditional school culture to one that welcomes learner voice and choice. Over multiple years, site leaders learn and refine strategies and protocols for their respective buildings; participate in application-based, transparent professional learning structures; and model learner voice and choice within these communities. These outcomes dovetail with district efforts to promote enhanced student and teacher self-efficacy, directly impacting an increasingly positive, collaborative learning environment.

The readiness indicators in figure 3.3 provide site administrator teams with milestones and look-fors that can inform long-term planning efforts. The three tiers of readiness supports identify communication structures, professional learning priorities, and data that can align to inform real-time progress.

The readiness indicators and supports we recommend for administrators are similar to those we outline for classroom educators. This is not accidental. A primary characteristic of an increasingly JEPL culture is an inclusive, *flat* environment that removes traditional hierarchical structures. Administrators, coaches, and teachers collaborate regularly during the course of a regular school day, week, month, and year. Again, many districts benefit from a close partnership with an external entity to handle the adult learning model shift through the first two to four years of implementation per our experience.

The District Administrator Role

A critical element that nurtures sustained and scaled changes in schools and districts involves the disciplined, committed application of protocols. A *protocol* in this context is a "set of step-by-step guidelines" that educators use to "structure professional conversations or learning experiences to ensure that meeting, planning, or group-collaboration time is used efficiently, purposefully, and productively" (Protocol, n.d.).

Administrators and classroom teachers across the United States use protocols in three fundamental ways.

Readiness indicators: To what extent are site administration teams measurably able to define, promote, and nurture opportunities for learner voice and choice? What practical and proven strategies correlate with increasing complexity levels in these regards?

Emerging Readiness Indicators	Moderate Readiness Indicators	High Readiness Indicators
• Site administration teams perceive district vision and mission for learner voice and choice from a compliance perspective. Their predominant question may be, How can my teachers practice limited strategies in this area? They do not yet see how access, JEPL, and personalization will catalyze a new learning framework. • The district defines and reinforces the roles within site leadership teams in traditional ways. Learner voice and choice may emerge as a priority in select schools, but only because that principal has identified them as a priority. • Site administration teams do not possess the knowledge, confidence, or buy-in to independently communicate the district vision and mission for learner voice and choice and JEPL. They require ongoing administrator-targeted professional development to help expand skills required to lead this work.	• Site administration teams understand that the district vision and mission for leader voice and choice and personalized learning represent a departure from the conventional learning model that pervades their existing school culture. They are open to support that helps them lead the shift between what exists and what will be. • Roles within site administration teams are enhanced to leverage district and external supports to establish the foundation for personalized learning and JEPL. District mandates that continuous school-improvement plan (CSIP) include leadership capacity–development plan among faculty. • Low-readiness school leadership teams demonstrate sufficient knowledge, confidence, and buy-in to independently communicate the district vision and mission for learner voice and choice, personalized learning, and JEPL.	• Site administration teams autonomously adjust their CSIP based on formative data from JEPL systems, technology access statistics, and changes in student learning as described through learning platform analytics. They share practice within and beyond the district community. • Site administration teams proactively and innovatively apply personalized learning and JEPL as catalysts for continual improvement. They nurture a pipeline of model classroom teachers to serve as hosts for visits and reflection. • Low- and moderate-readiness schools' site administration teams demonstrate sufficient knowledge, confidence, and buy-in to independently communicate the district vision and mission for personalized learning and JEPL.

continued →

Figure 3.3: Site administration team's readiness indicators and supports.

Emerging Readiness Supports	Moderate Readiness Supports	High Readiness Supports
• A cohort of forward-leaning principals and their site-based teams work with district and external providers to build the foundation to realize the vision and mission for personalized learning and JEPL. These schools receive advanced professional development so they may eventually serve as catalysts for scale and sustainability through courageous leadership and hard work.	• Administrators partner with one or two schools to share systems and experience as district scales its learner voice and choice initiative alongside its vision and mission for personalized learning and JEPL. An external provider launches and gradually releases facilitation of this paired schools model.	• All district schools engage in realizing the district vision and mission for personalized learning and JEPL. Site administration teams engage one another to share innovation, solve challenges, and crowdsource just-in-time solutions. Individual administrators emerge as thought leaders for the benefit of colleagues near and far.

Readiness supports: What structures, resources, and data are necessary to support site administration teams as they facilitate deeper and more frequent opportunities for learner voice and choice?

Emerging Readiness Supports	Moderate Readiness Supports	High Readiness Supports
• **Communications:** The district trains site administration teams to apply branding (logo, mascot, tagline, and hashtags) to pertinent school communications. District or professional development partners train all administrators to effectively communicate about the common language document to clarify and promote key terminology, dispositions, and skills. Administrators receive professional development on best practices associated with model classrooms and how to support teachers as they implement learner voice and choice outcomes. Attendees are tasked in future years with supporting additional administrator cohorts as a means of	• **Communications:** The district trains site administration teams to apply branding to all student, teacher, and parent communications that outline learner voice and choice, the personalized learning platform, and the four Cs (Partnership for 21st Century Learning, n.d.). Site administration teams apply language from the district crosswalk document among differentiated, individualized, and personalized learning descriptors in formative feedback rounds. Administrators leverage district-procured exemplars. Administrators promote model classrooms as centers for JEPL.	• **Communications:** Principals actively seek out potential case studies of innovative classrooms, community partnerships, and success stories of recent district graduates for branding. Leadership teams work with teachers to identify and share student work samples as artifacts of the district vision and mission around personalized learning. Administrators reinforce model classrooms as critical catalysts for JEPL, collaboration, and success.

- building leadership capacity within the district.
- **Knowledge and skills development:** The district provides JEPL to principals, assistant principals, and department and grade-level lead teachers on differentiation, individualization, and personalized learning. District and external partner align supports for spring and summer institutes on leadership professional development (for instance, developing digital citizenship culture, leading pilot schools, personalized and blended, and so on). Site administration teams participate in model classroom professional development with their selected teachers to maximize application of the common language document and JEPL structure.
- **Feedback mechanisms:** Data collected from stakeholder response to traditional and non-traditional promotions inform ongoing district messaging refinement. These data ascertain a baseline measure of how the common language document is perceived and used. The district selects and trains highly prepared, mobilized teachers and coaches in pilot schools and model classrooms.

- **Knowledge and skills development:** Site administration teams receive personalized learning training in multiple formats. Site administration teams take part in coaching for model classroom teachers. The district facilitates an expanding range of planning sessions for administrators on leading a culture of learner voice and choice, personalized learning, and the common language document. District or professional development partners facilitate a three-month virtual leadership course for district educators for continuing education credit. Administration teams receive JEPL to support the expansion of model classroom teachers at participating schools.
- **Feedback mechanisms:** Increased social media literacy occurs among site leadership teams. Tight CSIP integration occurs with model classroom, and learner voice and choice efforts align to district vision for personalized learning. The district gathers administrator feedback on virtual course participation and best practice application.

- **Knowledge and skills development:** Site administrators collaborate via the personalized learning platform to create learning content to scale district vision for personalized learning. Reflective Friends* or instructional rounds cohorts help administration teams reinforce best practice in their management of model classrooms across all school sites. Teams have a full, consistent range of professional learning options: large group, workshop, JEPL, and virtual. Teams develop CSIP outcomes that promote sustained, deep learning platform integration.
- **Feedback mechanisms:** The district gathers stakeholder response to traditional and untraditional promotions. It garners personalized learning platform competency-based data that describe adult and child learning growth. Coaches, administrators, and visiting teachers in model classrooms offer rich, multifaceted reflection.

*Per Henrico County Schools (2013), Reflective Friends are voluntary professional development teams.

Source: © 2014 by Advanced Learning Partnerships.

1. To maintain purposeful collaborative contact
    with colleagues

2. To reinforce professional voice in everyday decision
    making on instruction, curriculum, and assessment

3. To maximize their use of limited planning time

Educators can visit popular organizations like the National School
Reform Faculty (www.nsrfharmony.org) or the School Reform
Initiative (www.schoolreforminitiative.org) to access protocols that
support virtually any aspect of their professional, curricular, or assessment development.

Experienced and committed instructional coaches often play an
important role in establishing protocols in schools (The University of
Florida Lastinger Center for Learning, Learning Forward, & Public
Impact, n.d.). Districts and schools have a wide range of titles for this
position. For this book, we define *instructional coach* as a leadership role
facilitated by an experienced, successful educator who engages administrators and teachers in ongoing support that expands best practices,
reinforcing learner voice and choice.

Many districts now recognize the importance of developing an internal leadership pipeline for instructional coaches on a level of strategic
importance once reserved for aspiring principals and district administrators. Creating and implementing a professional learning sequence
for instructional coaches requires careful planning and third parties
often provide support. However, the return on this investment is a critical building block in the transition from a traditional catalog-based
professional learning structure to a more job-embedded, personalized
one. Their ability to attend to planning details such as communication,
logistics, and follow-up tasks maximizes the foundation on which a district introduces and reinforces protocol. Coaches who initially model
and then oversee the protocol's gradual release contribute significantly
to the sustainability of purposeful professional collaboration across all
grade levels. Most important, coaches who are available within a two-
or three-week window following a protocol-driven planning session to

support individual co-planning, team teaching, and reflection serve to maximize the implementation of key conclusions derived during the group meeting.

Protocols are a cost-effective and accessible tool for educators who recognize the potential that a group of committed colleagues can exert on its school community. The best protocols are simple, clearly defined processes that allow educators to engage in discovery, planning, reflection, and refinement in objective, collaborative ways. When introduced and supported by an instructional coach or trained educator, protocols have the potential to generate a reliable structure for educators to carefully incorporate opportunities for learner voice and choice. Grant Wiggins (2014) shares the story of a high school teacher who decided to walk in the shoes of a student for two days and reflect on the experience. The educator's conclusions highlight the passivity and exhaustion that traditional assignments and repetitive, low-level assessments generate. Since then, thousands of administrators and teachers have followed in these footsteps, validating these concerns and, more importantly prompting questions around the exploration of enhanced learner voice and choice in everyday curriculum and assessment. The Shadow a Student Challenge (http://shadowastudent.org)—in which educators select a student to observe for an entire day to gain better insight into how to improve the learning experience—is just one example of a reflective, protocol-driven approach to sustained learning.

An appropriately selected protocol, with district and administrator support and capable coach facilitation and reinforcement, can provide powerful structure for empowering learner voice and choice during a busy academic year. Our experience teaches us that a well-orchestrated protocol can spread quickly when participants reach out to their own networks and teaching teams with results of their success. For this reason, it is especially critical that site administrators engage in or at least are made aware of this collaboration from the outset.

Personalizing Through Example

Principal Paul House (Clear Creek Independent School District, Texas) invited Amos to visit seven classrooms in his high school with him and four students—a freshman, sophomore, junior, and senior. Amos facilitated a modified version of the Learning Walks protocol during these visits, which allowed Paul and his students to reflect on learner voice. Students predicted what questions the students they visited in those classrooms would ask if given the chance to query the teacher. Per the protocol, visiting students focused on aspects of voice and choice without being critical of the teachers who hosted their visits. They shared their experience with interested faculty, who worked to establish their own school-based protocol for inviting student participation in educator-driven planning sessions on instructional practice and department-level curriculum planning (personal communication, January 25, 2015).

Marsha Cale in Isle of Wight County Schools is working with her site administration and teachers to implement a project-tuning protocol she and the staff observed during a visit to High Tech High in San Diego. This thirty-minute protocol allows for a teacher to present a curriculum unit to a group of colleagues for review. Driven by established norms that ensure clarity, community, and precision, Marsha facilitated the protocol so that participating teachers can focus on collaborating with their team members. After successfully facilitating four project tunings, she cofacilitated project-tuning sessions with teachers who are eager and ready to assume leadership roles using this protocol (personal communication, November 16, 2016).

For five consecutive years, educators in Dubuque, Iowa, facilitated protocols associated with Authentic Intellectual Work framework during their regularly scheduled teacher team meetings. Each group consisted of approximately twelve educators, representing a wide range of pedagogical philosophies, grade levels, and content areas. While the focus changed each year, they aligned the charge to maximize student mastery of higher-order-thinking skills in all classrooms with the district's 1:1 technology initiative (J. Ross, personal communication, February 13, 2012).

At the Science Leadership Academy (https://scienceleadership.org) in Philadelphia, every student meets weekly with a mentor for four years. Those mentors help learners identify and set worthwhile goals, manage and monitor progress toward achieving those goals, learn from failure, and to celebrate success. They provide essential guidance to developing learners in environments that prioritize student voice (C. Lehmann, personal communication, November 4, 2016).

Other district leadership teams can accomplish a similar outcome. The readiness indicators in figure 3.4 (page 54) provide district executive teams with milestones and look-fors that can inform long-term planning efforts. The three tiers of readiness supports identify communication structures, professional learning priorities, and data that can align to inform real-time progress. Given their executive leadership roles, district administrators should have access to these readiness indicators as part of their overarching implementation plan to scale learner voice and choice. The executive team in Evergreen Public Schools refined a customized version of the following framework and shared it with a wide range of stakeholders to model co-authorship and earn trust (C. McMurray, personal communication, October 15, 2015).

One Last Story on Scale

As consultants and educators, all of us, the authors, have dealt with the million-dollar question, How do we build this to scale? We discuss many factors in this chapter that expose this work's sensitivity. Adam met with an educator whose focus on scaling personalized learning showed. She teared up as she reflected on and answered a question about her fears and hopes for this work. She said, "I think of my daughter starting her freshman year and all the other students we are missing by not providing an environment that allows them to think critically, problem solve, and be creative, and it breaks my heart. We have to do this work right, but we can't wait another minute" (J. John, personal communication, August 3, 2017). That is why this work is so important.

Readiness indicators: To what extent are district administrators measurably able to communicate, promote, and nurture opportunities for learner voice and choice? What practical and proven strategies correlate with increasing complexity levels in these regards?

Emerging Readiness Indicators	Moderate Readiness Indicators	High Readiness Indicators
• Critical district departments collaboratively plan to create implementation and communication plans for learner voice and choice as well as personalized learning rollouts.	• Critical district departments collaboratively manage implementation and communication plans for learner voice and choice and personalized learning rollouts. They establish feedback mechanisms to inform future adjustments.	• Critical district departments continually adjust implementation and communication plans for learner voice and choice and personalized learning rollouts based on accurate, real-time feedback from all stakeholder groups.
• District administrators nominate key district personnel as implementation and communication leads. Those leads align appropriate resources (time, outside support, and existing district structures) in accordance with realistic milestones across an initial eighteen-month time line.	• District administrators oversee implementation and communication plans. They optimize emerging feedback mechanisms based on initial rounds of data gathering. The district leadership team has access to regular updates against established milestones.	• Administrators deeply integrate ongoing implementation and communication plans into all district departments and structures. Transparent, reliable feedback mechanisms offer district leaders real-time data on areas of strength and emerging need.
• Administrators identify critical positions that will evolve to leverage the district vision and mission for learner voice and choice and personalized learning. District administrators work with external providers to establish a scope of work for facilitating a human resources analysis of specific roles to inform future profiles and professional development.	• District staff who occupy these critical positions receive high-quality professional development to support the adjusted role profile. The competency analysis for each position informs selection criteria for positions the district will fill within a candidate pool.	• The district fully mobilizes staff who occupy positions critical to the scaled implementation of both personalized learning and JEPL. Site leadership teachers and classroom teachers understand their roles well.
• Major district departments work with external partners to create a professional learning plan and customize the learning platform to allow for maximum systems	• District technology and curriculum and instruction departments achieve systems interoperability through the personalized learning platform. Curriculum coordinators and select department or grade-level chairs	• District technology and curriculum and instruction departments collaborate to scale all pertinent content through the ITS (an IMS) learning platform. This is synchronized with the district transition to JEPL,

interoperability. Curriculum coordinators emerge as the first platform experts and inform macro-level planning for curricular and assessment personalization. • District-level innovation concentrates on the development and reinforcement of an integrated implementation and communications plan. The key measure of quality is largely predicated on effective time and resource use to initiate needed organizational change, systems interoperability within the personalized learning platform, and a dynamic professional learning sequence.	co-develop, facilitate, and reflect on a range of personalized units and assessments with outside experts. Feedback from this process informs scaled development and launches future content. • District-level innovation expands to include an aspect of continuous improvement as defined through various feedback mechanisms. Systems-level data, which allow district leadership to adjust resources to amplify gains and mobilize assistance in areas of demonstrated need, define the key measure of quality. The personalized learning platform emerges as a critical value-add in this stage.	which allows district staff to sustainably support all stakeholder groups. • District-level innovation manifests into unanticipated formats. Opportunities to engage educators and students beyond the traditional confines of time and space emerge. A department of innovation may address new opportunities afforded within a personalized learning framework. The district administrators could activate new roles that individuals and groups of students, teachers, and administrators may take on.

Readiness supports: What structures, resources, and data are necessary to support classroom educators as they facilitate deeper and more frequent opportunities for learner voice and choice?

Emerging Readiness Supports	Moderate Readiness Supports	High Readiness Supports
• **Communications:** District leadership develops introductory, or splash, page for the website outlining vision and mission for learner voice and choice and personalized learning. The district establishes branding and social media protocols and applies	• **Communications:** District leadership consistently communicates key terminology, skills, and dispositions through all district communications to stakeholders. It carefully communicates enhanced role profiles for critical district personnel for the	• **Communications:** District leadership optimizes a district organizational chart to broker responsive personalized learning for adults and students. It clearly communicates and reinforces all associated processes are between district and school sites.

continued →

Figure 3.4: District administrator readiness indicators and supports.

them to site leadership professional development offerings. It communicates the process for reviewing critical district-level positions will be in multiple formats. The district creates regular videos and other untraditional media spots highlighting ongoing systems interoperability with personalized learning. Curriculum specialists share their learning with department and grade-level leaders in regular meetings. Curriculum specialists identify and mobilize key personnel and resources to support district communications plan.

- **Knowledge and skills development:** District leadership team works with external providers to create content for the district splash website and social media professional development for site leadership teams. Human resources leadership facilitates review of critical district positions via competency analysis and enhanced role profile documentation. District and learning platform partner work together to create video spots outlining systems interoperability. External provider

purposes of retention, professional development, and talent acquisition. The district showcases systems interoperability with the personalized learning platform in a sample lesson as well as unit and assessment plans in key grade levels and subject areas.

- **Knowledge and skills development:** The district develops, communicates, and continuously improves an eighteen-month, comprehensive professional learning plan based on stakeholder feedback. It fills critical district positions with capable, focused professionals who model best practices in JEPL and district vision for personalized learning in their work with site leadership teams, model classroom teachers, and general faculty. The district grounds teacher professional development in the increasingly sophisticated use of the personalized learning platform, and the district offers professional development across key grade levels and subject areas in multiple formats (institutes, JEPL, virtual, and model classrooms).

The technology and curriculum and instruction departments continually collaborate to enhance digital content and interoperability of systems through the learning platform. The district brands innovation as a critical element of continuous improvement.

- **Knowledge and skills development:** The district develops, communicates, and continuously improves an updated, comprehensive professional learning plan based on stakeholder feedback. Competency analysis for additional site-level positions (administrators, teachers, and non-certificated personnel) yields dynamic new role profiles that foster site-level innovation and rich interpretations of the district vision for personalized learning. Technology (including devices and the personalized learning platform) is ubiquitous and grounded in a fundamental level of stakeholder skill and comfort. Innovation emerges as a catalyst for continuous improvement and collaboration with cross-country districts.

facilitates the district needs assessment and assets inventory.

- **Feedback mechanisms:** District leadership gathers stakeholder feedback on emerging versions of the district splash website. An emerging social media presence appears across school sites. The district garners enhanced competencies and role profile documents for critical district positions. District leaders and external providers generate and present needs assessments and assets inventory reports to district leaders and school board. The district gathers stakeholder response to systems interoperability video spots. Key personnel associated with the district communications plan report are regularly in accordance to pre-established monthly milestones.

- **Feedback mechanisms:** The district soundly establishes a feedback loop associated with the district communications plan, and the plan draws on diverse, reliable sources. Social media presence at all schools meets minimum thresholds. Performance appraisal data for critical district personnel demonstrate reasonable growth in their first implementation year. Site leadership teams integrate aligned vision for learner voice and choice implementation, personalized learning, and model classrooms in CSIPs. Educator feedback and learning platform content repository demonstrate high-quality exemplars.

- **Feedback mechanisms:** The district integrates a feedback loop, associated with the district communications plan, in all implementation aspects. Social media presence at all schools exceeds minimum thresholds. Performance appraisal data for district and site-level critical district personnel demonstrate sustained growth across multiple implementation years. Technology and curriculum and instruction departments innovate and collaborate to draw on common continuous improvement data.

Source: © *2014 by Advanced Learning Partnerships.*

Epilogue
The Personalized Approach

We purposely started chapter 1 (page 7) and chapter 2 (page 21) describing students Erik Martin and Adora Svitak's experience, students who know their voices and use their choices to engage in learning ownership through many means, including embracing failure and creativity (TED, 2010; TEDxYouth, 2013). We address voice and choice in this book because they are the keys to students taking control of their own learning. Properly established within classrooms and schools at large, amplified student voice and choice can support changes that gradually allow for a true personalized approach to learning.

Personalized learning is something that every teacher can accomplish and, in some cases, is already accomplishing—and without a complex, multiyear path for implementation. Though we agree that other personalized learning components—pace, technology access, learning style, professional learning, learning spaces, and teacher as facilitator, for example—are important, so many other publications focus on those. We can't get to the personalized learning we propose without allowing students (as well as teachers and administrators) to use their voices to articulate their choices. Go include students in classroom, schoolwide, and districtwide choices. Empower teachers to be creative in their classrooms. Empower students.

We don't have a minute to waste if we are going to make sure that the next generation of students gets the education it needs and deserves. Commit to trying two or three things you've learned to empower students to personalize their learning and amplify their voice and choice.

References and Resources

Abel, N. (2016). *What is personalized learning?* Accessed at www.inacol.org/news/what-is-personalized-learning on May 2, 2017.

Ackoff, R. L. (1990). Redesigning the future: Strategy. *Systems Practice, 3*(6). Accessed at www.serresbiz.com/busedu/en/strategy-en/literature/1990_strategy.pdf on January 20, 2017.

Aslam, S. (2017). *Snapchat by the numbers: Stats, demographics & fun facts.* Accessed at www.omnicoreagency.com/snapchat-statistics on May 2, 2017.

Azzam, A. M. (2007). Special report: Why students drop out. *Educational Leadership, 64*(7), 91–93. Accessed at www.ascd.org/publications/educational-leadership/apr07/vol64/num07/Why-Students-Drop-Out.aspx on January 3, 2015.

Bill and Melinda Gates Foundation. (2014). *Early progress: Interim research on personalized learning—Report.* Accessed at http://k12education.gatesfoundation.org/resource/early-progress-interim-report-on-personalized-learning on October 5, 2017.

Bloom, B. S. (Ed.). (1956). *Taxonomy of educational objectives: The classification of educational goals; Handbook I: Cognitive domain.* New York: David McKay.

Bray, B., & McClaskey, K. (2014, June 25). *Updated personalization vs. differentiation vs. individualization chart version 3* [Blog post]. Accessed at www.personalizelearning.com/2013/03/new-personalization-vs-differentiation.html on January 23, 2017.

Bray, B., & McClaskey, K. (2016, May 9). *Continuum of self-efficacy: Path to perseverance* [Blog post]. Accessed at www.personalizelearning.com/2016/05/continuum-of-self-efficacy-path-to.html on January 23, 2017.

Busteed, B. (2013, January 7). *The school cliff: Student engagement drops with each school year* [Blog post]. Accessed at www.gallup.com/opinion/gallup/170525/school-cliff-student-engagement-drops-school-year.aspx on October 10, 2014.

Cazden, C. B. (2001). *Classroom discourse: The language of teaching and learning.* London: Pearson.

Children's Online Privacy Protection Act of 1998, 15 USC §§6501–6505.

Clayton Christensen Institute. (n.d.). *Blended learning definitions.* Accessed at www.christenseninstitute.org/blended-learning-definitions-and-models on January 9, 2017.

Content Science. (2016, August 23). *Influence: Millennial content consumption fact sheet.* Accessed at https://review.content-science.com/2016/08/millennial -content-consumption-fact-sheet on September 18, 2017.

Cotton, K. (2014). *Classroom questioning.* Accessed at http://educationnorthwest.org /sites/default/files/ClassroomQuestioning.pdf on September 19, 2017.

Depka, E. (2017). *Raising the rigor: Effective questioning strategies and techniques for the classroom.* Bloomington, IN: Solution Tree Press.

Dieker, N. (2016, July 26). *Infographic: The absolutely ridiculous amount of content consumed every minute.* Accessed at https://contently.com/strategist/2016/07/26 /infographic-content-consumed-every-minute-absolutely-ridiculous on November 9, 2016.

DIY Gamer Kit. (2017). Accessed at www.techwillsaveus.com/resources/diy-gamer -kit/unsoldered-manual on June 6, 2017.

Domonoske, C. (2016, November 23). *Students have 'dismaying' inability to tell fake news from real, study finds.* Accessed at www.npr.org/sections/thetwo-way /2016/11/23/503129818/study-finds-students-have-dismaying-inability-to -tell-fake-news-from-real on December 31, 2016.

DuFour, R., DuFour, R., Eaker, R., Many, T. W., & Mattos, M. (2016.) *Learning by doing: A handbook for professional learning communities at work* (3rd ed.). Bloomington, IN: Solution Tree Press.

Elmore, R. F. (2000). *Building a new structure for school leadership.* Accessed at http://files.eric.ed.gov/fulltext/ED546618.pdf on August 10, 2017.

Erickson, T. (2012, July 23). *The biggest mistake you (probably) make with teams.* Accessed at https://hbr.org/2012/04/the-biggest-mistake-you-probab on January 22, 2017.

Evergreen Public Schools. (2016). *Essentials of personalized learning.* Accessed at https://padletuploads.blob.core.windows.net/prod/113431986/e58e8eaa7 6342fab1cfc85124a697757/EPS_Essentials_of_Personalized_Learning.pdf on October 6, 2017.

Family Educational Rights and Privacy Act of 1974, 20 USC §§1232g.

Fogarty, R. (1994). *The mindful school: How to teach for metacognitive reflection.* Palatine, IL: Skylight Publishing.

Future Ready Schools. (2016). *Future ready framework definitions.* Accessed at http://futureready.org/wp-content/uploads/2016/07/FutureReadyFramework Definitions.pdf on July 17, 2017.

Gardner, H. (1983). *Frames of mind: The theory of multiple intelligences.* New York: Basic Books.

Hall, A., Medved, D., Beato, C., Malkin, B., & Liang-Vergara, C. (2017). *Communication and outreach strategies for leaders shifting to personalized learning.* Accessed at www.inacol.org/wp-content/uploads/2017/04/iNACOL-April-2017 -Leadership-Webinar.pdf on August 17, 2017.

Harress, C. (2013, December 5). The sad end of Blockbuster Video: The onetime $5 billion company is being liquidated as competition from online giants Netflix and Hulu prove all too much for the iconic brand. *International Business Times.* Accessed at www.ibtimes.com /sad-end-blockbuster-video-onetime-5-billion-company-being-liquidated -competition-1496962 on December 5, 2013.

Henrico County Schools. (2013). *Student 21.* Accessed at http://blogs.henrico.k12 .va.us/student21 on October 6, 2017.

Hewlett Foundation. (n.d.). *Deeper learning.* Accessed at www.hewlett.org/strategy /deeper-learning on June 6, 2017.

International Society for Technology in Education. (n.d.). *ISTE standards for administrators.* Accessed at www.iste.org/standards/standards/standards-for -administrators on June 19, 2017.

Kamenetz, A. (2016, May 31). *K–12: One student tries to help others escape a "corridor of shame."* Accessed at www.npr.org/sections/ed/2016/05/31/473240474 /corridor-of-shame on January 16, 2017.

Kohn, A. (1993, September). Choices for children: Why and how to let students decide. *Phi Delta Kappan.* Accessed at www.alfiekohn.org/article/choices -children on January 22, 2017.

Lahaderne, H. M. (1968). Attitudinal and intellectual correlates of attention: A study of four sixth-grade classrooms. *Journal of Educational Psychology, 59*(5), 320–324.

Learning Forward. (n.d.). *Standards for professional learning.* Accessed at https://learningforward.org/standards on June 6, 2017.

Marzano, R. (2012, August 20). *Clear learning goals set students up for success (Part 1): The power of Dr. Marzano's design question 1* [Blog post]. Centennial, CO: Learning Sciences Marzano Center. Accessed at www.marzanocenter.com /blog/article/clear-learning-goals-set-students-up-for-success-part-1 on January 22, 2017.

McCrindle. (2014). *Generation Z: Born 1995–2009.* Accessed at http://mccrindle .com.au/resources/Gen-Z-Claire-Madden_Infographic_McCrindle.pdf on February 1, 2016.

McLeod, S. (2014, December 22). We need schools to be different. *The Huffington Post.* Accessed at www.huffingtonpost.com/scott-mcleod/we-need-schools-to-be -dif_b_6353198.html on June 28, 2016.

Mendes, J. (2014, March 19). *How to promote metacognition in the classroom.* Accessed at www.readinghorizons.com/blog/how-to-promote-metacognition-in -the-classroom on August 10, 2017.

Metiri Group. (2008). *Measure of student engagement: What is the measure of student-engagement?* Accessed at http://metiri.com/services/digital-learning -measurement-evaluation-assessment-tools/measure-of-student-engagement -evaluating-student-engagement-in-schools on May 2, 2017.

Mishra, P., & Koehler, M. J. (2006). *Technological pedagogical content knowledge: A framework for teacher knowledge.* Accessed at https://pdfs.semanticscholar.org /977d/8f707ca1882e093c4ab9cb7ff0515cd944f5.pdf on September 19, 2017.

The National Board for Professional Teaching Standards. (2016). *What teachers should know and be able to do.* Accessed at www.nbpts.org/standards-five-core -propositions on August 17, 2017.

National School Reform Faculty. (n.d.). *Critical Friends Groups purpose and work.* Accessed at www.nsrfharmony.org/system/files/protocols/cfg_purpose_work_0.pdf on August 17, 2017.

New Hampshire Department of Education. (2016). *Moving from good to great in New Hampshire: Performance Assessment of Competency Education (PACE).* Accessed at www.education.nh.gov/assessment-systems/documents/overview.pdf on August 17, 2017.

Noonoo, S. (2012, June 12). *Flipped learning founders set the record straight.* Accessed at https://thejournal.com/articles/2012/06/20/flipped-learning-founders-q -and-a.aspx on July 30, 2017.

Northwest Regional Educational Laboratory. (2000). *Increasing student engagement and motivation: From time-on-task to homework.* Accessed at http:// educationnorthwest.org/sites/default/files/byrequest.pdf on August 10, 2017.

Partnership for 21st Century Learning. (n.d.). *Framework for 21st century learning.* Accessed at www.p21.org/about-us/p21-framework on June 5, 2017.

Patrick, S., Worthen, M., Truong, N., & Frost, D. (2017). *Fit for purpose: Taking the long view on systems change and policy to support competency education.* Accessed at www.inacol.org/wp-content/uploads/2017/06/CompetencyWorks-FitForPurpose-TakingTheLongViewOnSystemsChangeAndPolicyToSupportCompetency Education.pdf on August 17, 2017

Pendergrast, L. P., Layman, C., Butchart, C. G., & Moore-Mott, S. (2012, February). Ages and stages: Conflict resolution at Carolina Friends School. *Health and Healing in the Triangle, 14*(4). Accessed at http://healthandhealingonline.com /ages-stages-conflict-resolution-at-carolina-friends-school on October 5, 2017.

Pomeroy, S. R. (2014, February 6). *Multiple-choice tests hinder critical thinking. Should they be used in science classes?* [Opinion]. Accessed at www.forbes.com/sites /rosspomeroy/2014/02/06/multiple-choice-tests-hinder-critical-thinking-should -they-be-used-in-science-classes on January 23, 2017.

PowerDirector Mobile Video Editor—Bundled. (2017). Accessed at www.microsoft .com/en-us/store/p/powerdirector-mobile-video-editor-bundled/9wzdncrfj2cq on June 6, 2017.

Project Tomorrow. (2012). *Mapping a personalized learning journey—K–12 students and parents connect the dots with digital* (Speak Up 2011 National Findings K–12 Students and Parents). Accessed at www.tomorrow.org/speakup/pdfs/SU11 _personalizedLearning_Students.pdf on May 2, 2017.

Protocol. (2013, August 29). In S. Abbott (Ed.), *The glossary of education reform.* Accessed at http://edglossary.org/protocols on June 12, 2017.

Puentedura, R. R. (2013). *SAMR: A brief introduction.* Accessed at http://hippasus .com/rrpweblog/archives/2015/10/SAMR_ABriefIntro.pdf on June 5, 2017.

Richmond, E. (2014). *What happens when students control their own education?* Accessed at www.theatlantic.com/education/archive/2014/10/what-happens -when-students-control-their-own-education/381828/ on August 5, 2017.

Riley, B. (2014, June 19). *Don't personalize learning.* Accessed at http://kuranga .tumblr.com/post/89290487631/dont-personalize-learning on January 20, 2017.

Robinson, K. (2012). *Do schools kill creativity?* Accessed at www.huffingtonpost.com /sir-ken-robinson/do-schools-kill-creativity_b_2252942.html on January 5, 2017.

Rogers, K. D. (2016). *Bring your own device: Engaging students and transforming instruction.* Bloomington, IN: Solution Tree Press.

Rose, T. (2016). *The end of average: How we succeed in a world that values sameness.* New York: HarperOne.

Rowe, M. B. (1972). *Wait-time and rewards as instructional variables: Their influence on language, logic and fate control.* Paper presented at the annual meeting of the National Association for Research on Science Teaching, Chicago.

Russell, K., & Sisario, B. (2016, March 24). In shift to streaming, music business has lost millions. *The New York Times.* Accessed at www.nytimes.com/2016/03/25 /business/media/music-sales-remain-steady-but-lucrative-cd-sales-decline.html on May 2, 2017.

Sabrina, D. (2017, February 3). Rising trend: Social responsibility is high on millennials' list. *The Huffington Post.* Accessed at www.huffingtonpost.com /danielle-sabrina/rising-trend-social-respo_b_14578380.html on May 2, 2017.

Samuels, S. J., & Turnure, J. E. (1974). Attention and reading achievement in first-grade boys and girls. *Journal of Educational Psychology, 66*(1), 29–32.

Satell, G. (2014). A look back at why blockbuster really failed and why it didn't have to. *Forbes.* Accessed at www.forbes.com/sites/gregsatell/2014/09/05/a-look-back -at-why-blockbuster-really-failed-and-why-it-didnt-have-to/#4588a20e261a on May 2, 2017.

Schlechty, P. C. (2002). *Working on the work: An action plan for teachers, principals, and superintendents.* San Francisco: Jossey-Bass.

Schmoker, M. (2004). Learning communities at the crossroads: Toward the best schools we've ever had. *Phi Delta Kappan, 85.* Accessed at https://asge6130 -instructional-leadership.wikispaces.com/file/view/Learning communities at the crossroads_schmoker.pdf on January 01, 2017.

Schooling, P., Toth, M., & Marzano, R. (2013). *The critical importance of a common language of instruction.* Accessed at www.learningsciences.com/wp/wp-content /uploads/2017/06/Common-Language-of-Instruction-2013.pdf on August 17, 2017.

Skinner, E. A., Wellborn, J. G., & Connell, J. P. (1990). What it takes to do well in school and whether I've got it: A process model of perceived control and children's engagement and achievement in school. *Journal of Educational Psychology, 82*(1), 22–32.

Smarter Every Day [SmarterEveryDay]. (2015, April 24). *The backwards brain bicycle—Smarter every day* [Video file]. Accessed at www.youtube.com/watch?v =MFzDaBzBlL0 on January 23, 2017.

Stahl, R. J. (1994). Using "think time" and "wait time" skillfully in the classroom. *Eric Digest.* Accessed at www.ericdigests.org/19951/think.htm on May 2, 2017.

Stiggins, R. (2008, September). *Assessment FOR learning, the achievement gap, and truly effective schools.* Paper presented at the Educational Testing Service and College Board conference, Educational Testing in America: State Assessments, Achievement Gaps, National Policy and Innovations, Washington, DC. Accessed at www.ets.org /Media/Conferences_and_Events/pdf/stiggins.pdf on October 6, 2017.

Sturgis, C., & Patrick, S. (2010). *When success is the only option: Designing competency-based pathways for next generation learning.* Accessed at www.inacol.org/wp -content/uploads/2015/03/iNACOL_SuccessOnlyOptn.pdf on June 5, 2017.

TED. (2010, April 2). *What adults can learn from kids | Adora Svitak* [Video file]. Accessed at www.ted.com/talks/adora_svitak on September 18, 2017.

TEDxYouth. (2013, October 21). *How World of Warcraft saved me and my education: Erik Martin at TEDxRedmond* [Video file]. Accessed at www.youtube.com /watch?v=IBpcTw7pzJs&feature=youtu.be on May 2, 2017.

Thomas, P. E. (1999, May). *Critical thinking instruction in greater Los Angeles area high schools* (Doctoral dissertation). Azusa Pacific University, Azusa, California. Accessed at www.criticalthinking.org/files/Azusa%20Pacific%20University_opt.pdf January 01, 2017 on May 2, 2017.

Toshalis, E., & Nakkula, M. J. (2012). *Motivation, engagement, and student voice.* Accessed at https://studentsatthecenterhub.org/wp-content/uploads/2012/04 /Exec-Toshalis-Nakkula-032312.pdf on October 6, 2017.

The University of Florida Lastinger Center for Learning, Learning Forward, & Public Impact. (2016). *Coaching for impact: Six pillars to create coaching roles that achieve their potential to improve teaching and learning.* Oxford, OH: Learning Forward. Accessed at https://learningforward.org/docs/default-source/pdf/coaching-for -impact.pdf on June 2, 2017.

Vogler, K. E. (2008). Asking good questions. *Educational Leadership, 65.* Accessed at www.ascd.org/publications/educational-leadership/summer08/vol65/num09 /Asking-Good-Questions.aspx on May 2, 2017.

Walsh, J. A., & Sattes, B. D. (2011). *Thinking through quality questioning: Deepening student engagement.* Thousand Oaks, CA: Corwin Press.

Wiggins, G. (2014, October 10). *A veteran teacher turned coach shadows 2 students for 2 days—A sobering lesson learned* [Blog post]. Accessed at https://grantwiggins .wordpress.com/2014/10/10/a-veteran-teacher-turned-coach-shadows-2-students -for-2-days-a-sobering-lesson-learned on January 17, 2017.

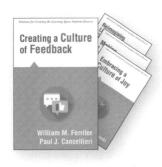

Solutions for Creating the Learning Spaces Students Deserve

Solutions Series: Solutions for Creating the Learning Spaces Students Deserve reimagines the norms defining K–12 education. In a short, reader-friendly format, these books challenge traditional thinking about schooling and encourage readers to question their beliefs about what real teaching and learning look like in action.

Creating a Culture of Feedback
William M. Ferriter and Paul J. Cancellieri
BKF731

Embracing a Culture of Joy
Dean Shareski
BKF730

Making Learning Flow
John Spencer
BKF733

Reimagining Literacy Through Global Collaboration
Pernille Ripp
BKF732

Different Schools for a Different World
Scott McLeod and Dean Shareski
BKF729

Personalizing Learning Through Voice and Choice
Adam Garry, Amos Fodchuk, and Lauren Hobbs
BKF657

GL⊙BAL **PD**

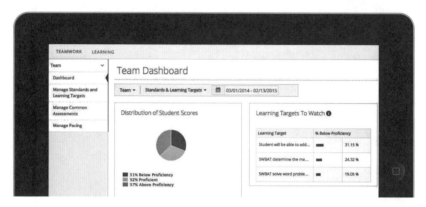

The **Power to Improve**
Is in Your Hands

Global PD gives educators focused and goals-oriented training from top experts. You can rely on this innovative online tool to improve instruction in every classroom.

- Get unlimited, on-demand access to guided video and book content from top Solution Tree authors.

- Improve practices with personalized virtual coaching from PLC-certified trainers.

- Customize learning based on skill level and time commitments.